IN TO ME YOU SEE™

A Story About Self Love and Healing

An Introduction to **The ITMYS™ Method**

Library of Congress Control number: 2024904149
ISBN: 979-8-9881746-7-7
Published by: Alegria Publishing
Book cover and layout by: @mckadamia

IN TO ME YOU SEE™

A Story About Self Love and Healing

An Introduction to **The ITMYS™ Method**

by Cinthia Gambino

TO MY TRIBE
whose purpose in my life has been to bring out the light
within that was hard for me to see

And

TO GOD, SPIRIT, THE UNIVERSE,
THE CONSCIOUSNESS
that vibrates for our greatest good and resonates in love
and wisdom through the collective.

This book could not have come to life without each and
every *"you got this"* that I so needed to hear.

In Love, Light, and Leadership

Cinthia Veronica Gambino

TABLE OF CONTENTS

ACKNOWLEDGEMENTS

Writing a book is not a solitary process. I am deeply grateful to the many individuals who supported me along this journey.

I want to express my gratitude to my family, both blood related and chosen, for your unwavering love and encouragement.

To my children, Kelly and Sebastian, I thank you for inspiring me every day with your boundless love and enthusiasm for life.

To my parents, Manuel and Virginia, and my siblings, Manny, Nick, Rodrigo, and Jesse. Your constant support has been my motivation to get to the finish line for all of us.

And, to my partner, Joffre, I thank you for providing a serene and quiet space for me to create.

Special thanks to Ana, Cristen, Wendy, Eva, Jenn, Chad and my teachers Vicky & Neal, for your insightful conversations on my story and **The ITMYS™ Method.** Thank you for always seeing me and allowing our Witnesses to connect beyond this realm to fulfill our purpose of changing the world for the greatest good and benefit of all.

To my medicine tribe and colleagues, I am indebted to you who provided invaluable feedback and encouragement.

I extend my appreciation to the Alegria Media and Publishing team, Davina and Charlie, for providing resources and support for my development, and your assistance in navigating the complexities of the publishing process.

I am deeply grateful to my editor, Jan Edwards, whose keen insights and meticulous attention to detail helped shape this manuscript into its final form.

I draw inspiration from countless authors, scholars, philosophers, spiritual and indigenous teachers whose work has influenced mine and paved the way for my own exploration.

Last, but not least, I want to express my gratitude to the readers who embark on this journey with me. Your support means more to me than words can express.

Thank you to each and every person who played a part in making this book a reality. I am profoundly grateful for your kindness, encouragement, and unwavering belief in me.

With deepest appreciation,

Cinthia Veronica Gambino

FOREWORD

Cinthia is like magic. I vividly recall our first meeting when she effortlessly engaged various groups in a leadership program we both attended. She drew everyone's attention with her vibrant energy. Little did I know then that I would later become her coach, and she would become my dear friend.

Having known Cinthia for over seventeen years, I know her as a constant force for discovery and curiosity, fully embracing life. From hanging on a trapeze to salsa dancing, from overcoming cancer to exploring remote corners of the world, she approaches each experience with openness.

Cinthia has always been a truth seeker, and her adventures have led her to this moment of speaking her truth and building awareness for the collective. Her deep intuition and knowledge are obvious, and I'm grateful that she's decided to share her journey with us through **The ITMYS™ Method** and her story.

Through her design of **The ITMYS™ Method,** Cinthia provides us with a framework that fits into our chaotic, day-to-day lives and empowers us to manage our spirits and minds, cultivate awareness, and remember our agency. The beauty of it lies in its universal applicability. Whether at work, at home with our partner, or at the park with our kids, we can apply what Cinthia has developed with **The ITMYS™ Method** to improve our lives.

The framework gives us tools that offer names and categories for the human and spiritual experience and a beautiful method of identifying when we are in each of those roles. This level of awareness not only allows us to center ourselves, but also expand the way we view ourselves and create the results we want.

Cinthia's gift to simplify complex feelings, theories, and thoughts makes this book a powerful guide for reconnecting with our true essence amidst life's tumultuous journey.

I extend my heartfelt gratitude to everyone who has supported Cinthia on this journey, including her devoted family and friends. I send love to our MITT familia, particularly our LP 68 familia, who have become like sisters and stood by Cinthia's side through every triumph and trial. And I thank the remarkable healers and shamans in Peru and other parts of the world, whose teachings have contributed to Cinthia's profound spiritual growth. She truly has done the work of finding her truth, and we are all blessed by it.

Thank you, Cinthia, for your continued commitment to living life to its fullest and providing us with a roadmap to do the same.

Wendy Amara,
Strategic Life & Business Coach

PREFACE

They say that your life is your story. If that's true, I've obviously not yet reached the end of mine. And, when I finally do, I won't be here to tell it as I understand it then. So, I'm telling it now, because I'm not going to die with my story still inside of me.

I can't imagine that God and the Universe would have brought all of those situations into my life for me to experience them alone and keep the knowledge to myself. I would like to believe that it serves a purpose bigger than just my existence. My hope is that the stories I share will prove that there has been purpose in all my experiences, including that of bringing this wisdom forth for others. My dream is to help us all expand and heal, so that we can continue the path of our lives from a practice of presence. Perhaps, my purpose is to lead others to a healing path of light and learning, through the practice of **The ITMYS™ Method.**

In To Me You See™ ~ The ITMYS™ Method came to me as a gift from my higher self for dedicating my life to the practice of heart-centered intention. It is written for you, the leader– *whether you're the parent, the child, the manager, the teacher, the aspiring coach, or the leader of your own life and trajectory.* It is here to help you step into being the heart-centered leader who creates and lives with awareness and purpose.

Please don't let the word "leader" give you pause. I had no vision of myself leading anyone. I was just a girl who felt different and tried to make sense of myself in the world. You will see those aspects of yourself in me, and in the most normal life a person could have. I think you will find resonance in reading the experiences that shaped my existence and eventually enabled me to understand what this whole ride of life is about. Your perspective on these may be similar to mine. It may provide insight that can support you, or someone you know, in navigating a situation. My story may compel you to conclude that life is merely a collective human experience designed to stretch us, break us down, strengthen us, and then re-shape us in a new way. Perhaps, it may even inspire you to share your story with others. My sense is that it will be all of these.

Within my story, the revelation of **The ITMYS™ Method** came as a direct result of my experiences. Discovering it changed my life and the lives of others, and it continues to do so. In reading these pages, you will gain understanding and a new awareness of how I used the tools presented in this book to find a way to overcome the adversities and traumas in my life. With this new awareness, you can incorporate the knowledge into your life and move forward with a new vision. Additionally, you can use the tools to communicate with your family, your loved ones, your partners, your subordinates, your teammates, your friends, and any relationships in a way that eases and inspires a truer connection with them.

Love and light is what we are all made of. We are not separate. We are all capable of connecting to the Source of this light that we come from and will return to when we leave our human vessels. Though our time here is but a glimpse, it is a journey of remembering, and a reminder to all of us when we have forgotten our origin and our purpose.

Maybe my purpose for writing this book is to be that reminder.

PRIVACY DISCLAIMER

INTRODUCTION

In revisiting my past, I sometimes wonder who the heck I was at the time. This makes sense, because I was a completely different person. In recognizing this, I ponder how many opportunities each of us gets to be what we want to be, how many shots we get at living the human experience. I don't imagine this is my first go-round. Maybe I didn't complete my previous assignment, and this is my opportunity to fulfill my purpose.

Years ago, had I been told that I would become the woman and coach and community sister I am today, I would have not believed it. Yet, here I am, living this life of magic and synchronicities, manifestations and beauty, and love and hope. I cannot even begin to describe the gratitude I feel at my ability to embrace everyone who comes into my life. And I can do that because I SEE them. I see their beauty and their struggle. It is a gift to feel the vibration of another person and connect with my desire to simply love them, help them heal, understand them, and feel unconditional love.

We are being called to embrace all aspects of ourselves, without shame, without fear, and without judgment. This is the path that can enable us to live out the trajectory of our lives from a story of our own writing, from an intentional space, called the WITNESS.

It is my recommendation that, in reading this book, you go deep and take the time to gain the gift of higher vision for yourself. From this higher place, you can then recognize the unconscious aspects that have created your reality, and begin to shift into the consciousness that creates a different reality, the one you want. This is the opportunity to design your new human existence.

As you reach the end of each chapter, you'll find a section called, Chapter Insight - Going Deeper. I invite you to take the time to go deeper than just my story. Perceive yourself and others there, and understand what is below the surface of our actions and emotions. You will begin to see the mirrors and reflect on the three different aspects of yourself and others. It is in these insights that you can see the unconscious, but powerful influence of these aspects on your past and present. And, this will allow you to shift the way you see yourself and the future you create for yourself.

In gathering these insights and carrying them with you across the bridge into the final chapter of the book, all the pieces will come together. You may even find yourself inspired to begin putting the insights into practice, so that you can consciously and intentionally create the next chapter of your life. If so, there is a gift that awaits you at the end, to help you do just that.

Your life is about the journey, not the destination. And that's not just some grandiloquent expression. Life is our experience in each moment and the wisdom gained from those experiences in the spaces and places we find ourselves. So, I'm going to share my story in places and spaces. Let's go back to 2008, when I had an experience that helped me remember why I came here.

PROLOGUE
From the Light

Typically, stories are shared from the beginning. However, perspective doesn't work that way. Understanding doesn't happen immediately in the moment. As they say, *"Hindsight is 20/20."* My mind tends to make sense of things more when I look at how the story ended, or when I'm standing at the junction, looking back.

For quite some time, I was working with a mentor in hypnotherapy training. In 2008, I had the honor of her guidance in a life regression experience. Life Regression is a spiritual journey that takes you backward in time, before you were born.

As I surrendered to the guidance, I found myself in the space of the collective consciousness, an expansive vibration of energy and light. I knew that I was me, but I wasn't just me. I was connected to all of the other souls, with no separation between me and them. We were all in one vibrational light, all energy.

Somewhere above and out in this space, we heard the voice, God-Spirit, say, *"The baby's about to be born."* All different scenarios of family lives were presented to us, and in the next moment, the life presented was the family I now belong to. We saw that a soul was about to go into that life, a female going in to be part of that family. We were shown it would be facing a life full of challenges, and were told they needed a soul that was willing to go in to face the adversities and be in partnership with the female mother, for the purpose of moving the family forward.

It was a huge assignment. *"You must be ready and willing to face these challenges."* I saw myself saying, *"I'll go."* The voice, God-Spirit, said, *"Alright."* And with that, I was assigned.

I saw myself coming in to the life experience of the woman laying on a birthing table. In seeing her suffering, I recognized my mother. I, as a Spirit Light came right in front of her face and said, *"I'm here, and we're going to do this together."* Her eyes were closed, and she was really struggling, writhing back and forth in pain. I said, *"We're going to do this together. I'm here to be your partner."* She agreed, and I agreed. I said, *"Okay"* and felt my soul entering into the fetus' body.

I immediately felt the sensation of becoming human, all senses coming alive, and I felt the weight of having a body. Then, I felt my human body being delivered out of my mother.

In my life regression experience, I understood that being a human is an opportunity for the soul to come to earth and humanity, to be a witness and to guide the human in the experiences that will allow him or her to complete whatever life assignment he or she came for.

At some point very early in life, we begin to become programmed by the human stories, thoughts, wounds, and judgments. And we soon forget who we really are and why we are here.

PART ONE

JOURNEY TO MYSELF

VIAJE HACIA MI

1

In the Stars - *En las Estrellas*

As is so with any universal truth, the knowing that we are connected to others came very naturally to me. Even as a young child, I knew that looking into someone's eyes would give me insight into who that person was. My dad said that he had to watch me constantly. When someone looked at me, I knew right away if they were pure. If they were, I immediately befriended them and went wherever they were going.

I was also curious, always asking questions. When I first asked my mother about my birth and the details of that day, she took the time to tell me about the night I was born.

Her labor had been challenging and lasted for hours. In Mexico, in those times, neither the father, nor the family was allowed inside the birthing room, so they were surprised when the doctor came out. My mom's struggle had become so extreme, to the point of dangerous, because of the difficulty and amount of blood loss, that the doctors left the birthing room and went into the waiting room to ask my father who he wanted to choose, his wife or his child. Without hesitation, my father answered, *"Quiero a las dos" ("I want them both")*. With that intention leading them, the doctors headed back into the birthing room and saved both my mother and me.

She recalled that her recovery roommate, a beautiful woman, whose nickname was "La Negra" (a term of endearment for Afro-Latin women), had also just given birth. In sharing the room and the experience of bringing a human into the world, they became friends and shared their stories of childbirth and life in general.

Between their conversations, in silent contemplation gazing out the window at the night sky, my mother noticed three stars that were brighter than the rest and formed a straight vertical line. Their light made such an impression on her that she called to "La Negra" to look. As they stared at the bright light in the dark sky, the three stars suddenly shot out in different directions, like fireworks. In disbelief, my mother asked, *"Vistes eso?" ("Did you see that?")*. "La Negra" did indeed.

My mother shared this story with me to remind me that something up there, out there, was looking out for me. She felt that the star display was confirming the success of my birth, overseeing that everything turned out as planned.

I had one older brother, Manny, and twin brothers, Nick and Rodrigo, who were six years my junior. My dad had eleven siblings, and my mom had ten, six of whom were women. We spent the majority of our time with my mom's family, mostly because her youngest sister was close in age to my older brother and me.

Our childhood was simple and wholesome, without many outside influences. We felt cared for in the connection and closeness nurtured by the elders. My dad's mother took care of us while our parents worked. Some of my greatest memories revolved around food. Both my parents were great cooks, and most of our meals were cooked for us. My mom made fresh chilaquiles, tostadas, and pozole, while dad made the more creative and delicious meat dishes and saucy "caldos" (stews). We were blessed with the good fortune of having fresh handmade flour tortillas each day. My grandmother rolled them right off the hot "comal" (griddle) and smeared them with fresh butter and homemade cheeses.

On hot sunny days, we played outside on the streets of the neighborhood until dark, riding our bikes and playing hide and seek, while the elders, our aunts and uncles, sat on the porch watching. Summer weekends were spent driving up to Ensenada and Tijuana to enjoy the fresh seafood served by the restaurants and vendors along the sandy beaches. During the week, most people focused on earning their living through their trades and talents, and we got to experience the fruit of their creative works at the "sobreruedas" (farmers' markets and flea markets on wheels). Seeing how people made a living by doing what they loved and selling just about anything made me wonder how one decided what to become as an adult, and how I would make my own path as I got older.

My parents designed and built our three bedroom home from the ground up, one brick at a time. Our neighborhood of La Independencia in Mexicali, Baja California was new when we moved there and still being built, so the roads were rusty red dirt. I recall my mom watering the newly planted trees outside of our home on summer evenings. She watered the road at the same time, to keep the dust down. The smell of the wet dirt was heaven to me, its clean mineral-rich scent lingering in my senses.

Looking back, I think that's where my affinity for rain and wet dirt came from. When I'm surrounded by it, my memory conjures up nostalgic thoughts of home, surrounded by dirt and land.

The yard around our home was lined with rose bushes of all colors. When she was a child, my mom dreamed of having a home where she could plant rows of rose bushes. She told us of how, in her childhood, she intentionally took a specific route home from school, so that she could pass the house that was surrounded by all the varieties of roses. Mexicali has a very hot desert climate, but her vision of having a garden and maintaining her childhood dream motivated her to take special care of the plants. She planted only those that thrived in the heat.

Our family was Catholic. Anything not Catholic was said to be bad or evil or of the devil, except for the special abilities of my mom's sisters. Their husbands referred to the seven as "The Cortes Sisters," because they possessed "witch-like" abilities. They were all intuitives who sensed things and had premonitions of circumstances that ended up happening. They were connected to Spirit. Those kinds of abilities were accepted and highly regarded, because they were the act of God giving a message through you. However, any other kind of divinity, like card reading was of the devil.

There were definite rules of behavior and conversation. At an event, a friend of the family told me that I was pretty, and I said, *"Thank you."* My mom immediately scolded me, *"You don't say that! You're not supposed to say that."* I was a kid, and no one had ever told me that. My natural response was to thank them for seeing me and letting me know. However, I was told right away that I was not supposed to say thank you. We were supposed to be humble and demure. There was always a behavioral judgment and feeling of comparison that was very clearly leading the code of behavior, like a dress code.

By the time I was seven, being raised under the influence of the code and judgment, as well as the witch-like intuitives, I had lived a lifetime of experiences. The cumulative effect made me feel very self-conscious and influenced me to dim my light, as well as my inner knowing abilities. I grew hesitant to be openly self-expressive, out of a fear of being judged, both by friends and family. I also had an inner knowing of when to trust people and when not. If I shared what I innately understood about spirituality or connectedness to Spirit, I would be judged for it or seen as odd. I remember receiving a confirmation of this with my childhood friend.

The evenings of Mexicali were much cooler than the days and, being far from any of the big cities, the dark night skies were brightly lit with stars. On one very memorable summer evening, my friend and I were laying on the truck bed of my father's faded red Datsun, staring up at the stars and the electric cables running from the poles that had recently been installed by the city to bring electricity to the community. They obstructed what had previously been a clear view to the stars, but we remained focused on them anyway, contemplating what was out there.

For a moment, I forgot that I was a child who had just been playing outside all day with all the neighbors. I sensed an instinctual pull within me, a surge of energy, and the skin on my body, around my arms, and on my belly grew prickly. The sensation was foreign to me, but I knew that the energy I was feeling was not coming from my body.

My eyes suddenly blurred with tears, both of connection and sadness. I felt connected with my friend lying next to me, connected to the energy of others around me, and connected to the stars. But, I had grown up knowing that others could not feel what I was feeling. The sadness I was feeling was their sadness from the separation they felt, the feeling of not being connected.

I didn't know what to make of the inner knowing I had that I was not separate from others, but the inter-connectedness made sense to me. I felt the connection to something bigger, something or someone outside of me, some energy form.

I started to explain to my friend that angels and guides communicate with us by showing us signs and giving us warnings and messages. She turned to look at me for a moment and then looked up in the direction I was looking, and then shifted her position. I could sense her loss for words. So, we laid there staring at the stars. I waited to hear a response from her, but it never came. She just stared out into space with me.

What became clear to me was that I was aware that there was something bigger than our bodies that connect-ed us, and her reaction provided the intel that I should never speak about it again. The silence of that night became a warning that what I was feeling, or seeing, or knowing was not a subject I should bring up with people. My friend never brought up that experience in all the years to come, and I knew not to either.

Chapter Insight - Going Deeper

If we dive deeper and look at our behaviors, commu-nications, thoughts, and emotions, we can begin to detect three aspects operating within each of us. The first is the inner voice, the storyteller that is constantly narrating what's going on. The second is the inner judgment that evaluates and assigns things and people as good, bad, right, wrong, normal, weird, enough, too much, etc. In doing so, it influences our storytelling, our beliefs, our choices, and our experiences. The third is the unattached neutral observer, the higher self watching high above it all, from a heart-centered knowing state.

When I was brought to tears from the immensity of my connection to the stars and everyone and everything, I was experiencing it from the point of view of my observer/higher self aspect.

Do you remember a period of your life when you felt this connection to the earth, people, Spirit, or all that is?

Beginning at about age seven, I began to feel a stronger and stronger influence of an inner judgment aspect and a storyteller aspect that aligned with the judgment and stories I was learning from others, about myself, about life, and about others. In the process, my natural observer/higher self that I had been connected with from birth grew more and more silent. In becoming self-conscious, mistrustful of people, and afraid to be openly self-expressive, because I would be judged, I began operating from the judgmental viewpoint of those I had been influenced by. Can any part of you relate to this from your childhood?

As I shared my knowing with my friend and felt her reaction, knowing that she did not feel what I felt, or understand me, I felt her judgmental aspect, even if she did not say a word. Have you ever experienced this?

2

Witchcraft - *Brujería*

The way my friend responded on that summer night imprinted on me a sense of separation. She showed me that I should not share my insights and senses. That experience defined my future interactions with others.

Nevertheless, I knew that I was able to see and feel things in a deeper way than I could explain or openly share with others, which aroused my curiosity about the neighbor across the street. She was different from the rest of the neighbors. My mom said that she was into dark magic. I didn't know what dark magic was, but knew that it couldn't be good. It seemed that anything dark was evil, like hidden energies lurking in the **shadows** of a dark room.

Observing her as she killed chickens outside her house only solidified that assumption in my developing mind. I watched one day from our living room window. With one quick thud of the knife as it met the wood of the tree trunk, the chicken's neck was severed. She held the chicken's head in her hand while its body scurried on the ground, not knowing yet that it was dead. As if she knew that I had been watching, she looked my way and saw me. Witnessing that, sparked my curiosity about what dark magic was and how she had sensed that I was watching. More importantly, I wondered, if she could make animals do that with their heads cut off, what could she do to humans.

During mass, I heard the church speak of prophecies, rituals, sacrifices, and the way miracles happened. I recall my mom dealing with situations around our house when the energy felt out of sorts, which she sensed was dark magic, or evil lurking. One of those situations occurred the day our family came home to find our path covered in dried egg.

Our house had a short walkway from the gate to the porch that was lined by rose bushes. The walkway led to a concrete porch, which was big enough to set our small plastic pool on in the summer or even ride bikes. So, it was a fairly big area. We first saw the egg on the walkway when we opened the gate, and then noticed that it went all the way onto the porch.

As soon as my mom saw it, she told us not to step on it. But, it wasn't soon enough to prevent my dad from stepping right onto it. Mom promptly walked around to the other side of the gate and turned the hose on the dried egg to clear it as well as she could. The rest of us entered through the other gate, to avoid stepping on the remnants.

My mother didn't say it, but it was clear to her that someone had cast "un mal" (an evil) spell against us, to bring ruin. Soon afterward, my dad had a quite significant car accident. His hip and both legs broke, and he was bedridden for months. Mom took a job to make ends meet, and my siblings and I stayed home to take care of our dad. As a result of his incapacitation, his business suffered, which quickly took a toll on our family's finances, and providing for our needs became more challenging. Mom attributed our downfall to our dad walking on the egg.

The theory behind an "un mal" cast on someone is that the caster's envy is intense enough to create a spell to cause ruin to the recipient. This is similar to the belief of "hacerle mal de ojo" (giving someone the evil eye), or touching someone's hair or possessions with such intense desire that the item would fall into ruin. Spells are ritualized to ensure that something will fail, especially if someone has intense jealousy for another's life, attributes, or possessions.

Whether it was the beautiful marriage my mom and dad had, or his successful business, or the good that he did for the community, whoever had cast that spell on our family envied what we had, enough to want to take our success away from us.

This experience made me realize that a person could have the ability to connect with another person's energy in a way that would affect the other person. Being exposed to these and other experiences and beliefs at a young age began to attune me to spirituality at a very formative time of my life. I was given a first-row seat at the school of curses, recognizing them and breaking them. As my curiosity continued to grow, and as I was later exposed to the spiritual beliefs and rituals of other areas of the world, I discovered that these spells are not unique to the Mexican population.

Shortly after the incident with the egg on the porch and my father's accident, my parents sought out a way to clean up "el mal." In her search, Mom was led to a bonafide "Brujo" (male witch). They thought that he might have, in fact, been the Brujo that the spellcaster had consulted to put the curse on our family. My mom had always been a fierce protector of those she held dear, so she gathered my father and brothers and me to go see him.

His office was decorated with plants, a selection of jeweled figures, gold crosses, saint-adorned candles, and various images of still faces. They could have been saints, or deities, and they were mostly serious or melancholic. We sat in front of and across from the Brujo as he sat at a regular looking desk and spoke with our mother. Unfortunately– *or fortunately, depending on which way you look at it*– he would not disclose any information about the identity of the spellcaster. However, he offered to help us to either reverse the "mal," or cast a protection spell over our family. In order to do that, he first needed to determine whether the curse was placed on our whole family, or on only one of us.

As I looked at the eyes of the images, the Brujo's voice caught my attention. He asked my mom for a picture of my dad, to test whether he had been affected by the spell. I watched intently as he set a glass of water and dark powdery mix in front of us and dropped the picture of my dad into the solution. It floated and then quickly sank to the bottom, as if it had been pushed by someone's finger. According to the Brujo, my father was the target.

Mom's face looked seriously puzzled, incredulous about what she had just witnessed and the decision she then had to make. If she had faith in God, and if she knew that God existed, which she did, she knew that evil also existed. It had been confirmed in front of our eyes.

As a seven-year-old child, what I saw greatly intimidated me, but my twin brothers were only two or three. I can't imagine the effect it had on them, or how it affected my older brother. I held on to my mother for reassurance, as we walked out of his office and into a dimly lit room. An elaborate altar presentation of the occult spanned an entire wall of images of various saints, deities, and other sinister looking images. The Brujo closed the door behind us and proceeded to invoke a ritualistic chant.

The six of us knelt before the altar, facing the Brujo. After completing his chant, he picked up a live rooster with one hand and held it in the air above a dirty white bucket. His other hand picked up a sharp looking blade and held it at the rooster's neck. The animal was squirming for freedom, but the Brujo held on tightly and whispered softly before sliding the blade smoothly across the base of its neck. We watched its squirming stop, as the life force left its body, and we heard the stream of the liquid blood drain into the bucket. The Brujo placed the lifeless corpse at the foot of the altar and turned to us. At that moment, I imagined that he would soon be cutting into our skin as well, or something of the sort.

With the blood of the rooster on his hand, he approached each of us, one at a time, claiming protection over our family, and smearing warm blood cross markings onto our foreheads and other parts of our bodies. My recollection of the details at this point are hazy. Either I intentionally forgot them, or what happened next was too intense for my mind to recall.

We never found out for sure if the neighbor Bruja was the one who cast the spell, but she and my mom had always had it out for each other. Regardless, after that, the curse lifted and things improved for our family.

My parents seldom talked about that incident. Nor have my siblings and I ever brought it up. My mom has shared that she felt guilty for going against the faith of the Catholic doctrine. She had always conducted herself as a devout Catholic, and a woman of faith, and kept her integrity intact and her words and actions pristine. Looking back, she repeatedly tried to forgive herself for that and viewed it as an act of fear and desperation, to protect our family in a weak moment.

For me, that experience opened the door for the deepening curiosity bubbling within me to expand. I became even more enticed and aware of what my parents referred to as "brujeria" (witchcraft), "espiritualidad" (spirituality), "angeles" (angels), "fantasmas" (ghosts), "profecias" (prophecies), and "Dios" (God). In my desire to know more about these entities and the realm of what was unseen to most, I started to see evidence of my parents' intunement with the spiritual world. I listened intently to them speak about their lives, and I picked up wisdom from their stories.

I noticed how my father jokingly called my mom and her side of the family "Brujas" (witches). He was also aware of special abilities of his own and often claimed that he was one degree away from being a Wiseman, *"Me falta un grado para ser sabio."* My father had many experiences that could not be explained by logic or rational reality. In reflecting on his life's desires, he said, *"Todo lo que he querido se me ha cumplido"* ("Everything I have ever wanted has come to be.").

I paid close attention to what my parents' beliefs and manifestations meant and the manner in which they practiced them. Through my desire to learn how they had this knowledge, I came to realize that it wasn't a practice or an action. It was the working of their subconscious in connection with the energy. My parents spoke things into existence. The older I became, the more quickly I recognized these manifestations.

My mom said things before they happened. She gave sudden warnings that seemed dramatic and drastic, as if she pulled random ideas out of the air– *except they were true.* Whatever warning she had spoken literally happened exactly as she said it would. We could not deny that she was right.

This taught me to question which came first, like the chicken or the egg, my mom's prediction, or the event that she could not see but knew. I wondered how much of it was already in motion before she spoke it, or how much of it was actually being formulated because she was speaking it into form. Or, even prior to that, I wondered if she was formatting it in her mind and, thereby, causing it to manifest before our eyes, before she even spoke it. All of this flamed the curiosity inside me and my yearning to learn more and how.

From a young age, watching my parents' behavior taught me that we had a connection to an unknown realm that listened to our words and thoughts and responded with physical appearances. As part of our nightly practice, Mom sat by our bedside, enacting the rituals and praying to our guardian angels. I knew that this was part of our conversation with this realm, and I wanted to understand who my angel was, and why an angel existed just to look out for me. I wanted to know how and why we prayed to the Virgin Mary and Jesus and God. So many questions sparked my young mind, all asking to recognize these entities we could not see, who listened to us, protected us, and granted us wishes.

I was confused about what or who was actually listening to my thoughts and prayers. I wanted to connect directly with them. Without knowing how or why or who, I prayed to all of them. I asked for them to deliver things, to test their existence. I witnessed things unfold in my favor, or magically come to be. Somehow, I knew that if I thought of something specific and became so certain that it would happen, inevitably it would happen. This was a new awareness, and I was not completely in tune with my own ability or empowerment yet.

It was about that time when I started to wonder who the chicken-killing neighbor was praying to and who the Brujo had called into that room as he chanted and whispered and sacrificed the rooster. I wanted to know which angels needed live sacrifices and why my prayers could be heard more powerfully if I offered the angels a sacrifice. Mostly, I wanted to know how to connect with the light and the dark.

During these early years of my life, the energies of magic became truly real for me, and I could not wait to learn more about the angels among us and the magic around us.

Chapter Insight - Going Deeper

If we look more deeply at the three aspects of the spellcaster, we can see that she was acting under the influence of her inner judgment when she cast the spell, an aspect based out of fear and evaluations that aren't true. She was also acting under the influence of her inner voice, telling the story that our family had too much. Believing that story, whether it was true or not, influenced her to envy us and react offensively by lashing out. Have you, or someone you know, acted on a belief or story, without knowing if it was actually true?

It takes two to make a spell or energetic intention affect someone, the offender and the defender. Both have to be engaged and focused on the situation with a belief (story) that it is real. The spell was able to work, because my mother and father engaged with it, reacted, sought defense, and believed in the story that they both were creating, which are the aspects of the inner judgment and the inner voice telling the story.

However, the Bruja was able to cast the spell by using her ability to connect with my family's energy. This ability is given by the objective observer/higher self, which is in connection with the energetic realm. Do you see this aspect in yourself, or anyone you know, or people you don't know?

My mom sought out the Brujo (the male witch), because she believed that he could connect with the energetic realm and create an action that would change the energy. And it did, because the Brujo knew how to connect with the other person, in a way that enabled him to "see" what had happened, as well as what energetic action to take to create the protective energy.

He knew all of this, because he had access to all of his aspects, the inner voice/storyteller, the inner judgment, and the objective observer/higher self. Many healers and energy workers have a level of awareness that enables them to access that energetic realm.

Have you noticed, or can you look back and see how the inner voice/storyteller and inner judgmental aspects were created or developed in you and others? Both the storyteller and judgmental aspects are created and shaped by society and other influences, for the purpose of controlling us– *making us unaware and unconscious of our true abilities and light and spiritual power.* The result is that we feel insecure, competitive, envious, unworthy, unlovable, depressed, powerless, and afraid.

If we can see ourselves, others, and our circumstances through our objective observer/higher self aspect, it is because we are accessing a Divine heart-centered intimacy, the central power of love that connects us all. When we do, we have a sense of peace and calm, because there is no falsely created need to run or hide, compare or compete, or win or fight. Have you noticed yourself in that space? When?

Both my mother and the Bruja could have viewed the situation from their objective observer/ higher self aspects, which would have resulted in each of them observing without reacting. This would have allowed them to access the aspect of heart-centered intimacy and connect with one another, rather than disconnect and offend (the Bruja) or defend (my mom). In this neutral observer state, the Bruja would have been able to perceive the good that my family was bringing to the community with a business that gave people jobs, community, financial abundance, and convenience through the products my parents were selling at the factory.

But my mom and the Bruja could only have done this had that aspect been developed enough and strong enough in each of them.

An underdeveloped observer/higher self aspect can be wrongfully influenced by an overly identified and conditioned inner judgment or voice/storyteller.

Because the objective observer/higher self aspect was underdeveloped in both my mom and the Bruja, they were easily influenced and manipulated by the inner storyteller and judgment. Since, my mom's observer aspect was underdeveloped, her inner voice told the story that others wanted to hurt her, and she viewed the Bruja as threatening and dangerous. However, the objective observer aspect was strong enough to give her the knowing that an energetic attack of some kind had taken place. But, she was unable to connect more deeply with it.

This part of my life was my introduction to the observer/higher self aspect of me and my first glimpse of how to access it. It showed me that I could go beyond the limited inner judgment and voice/storyteller aspects of myself and embrace my observer/higher self. My exposure to the cultural and spiritual beliefs and experiences of my family helped me develop my observer/higher self aspect. It also guided me to understand that connecting to this aspect is what gives me access to Spirit.

This is why those who have highly developed their observer/higher self aspect are able to proclaim things, predict things, call things into existence, and connect to each other. This is accessing in-tuition. Though it's spoken of as if we're connecting to something "out there," connecting to Spirit is an "in-tu" process.

3

Belonging - *Pertenecer*

By my ninth year, my youngest brother Jesse had decided to come into the world, so our family expanded to seven. When we, the Gambinos, were invited to family gatherings, we made the party. This was sometimes a joyful celebration, and a challenge at other times.

Latinos have a way of dropping by without invitation, or because they "happen to be driving by." During times like those, when we spontaneously stopped by the home of one of our family members, my dad stayed in the car with my siblings, while my mom and I tested the waters. After we knocked on the door, if the invitation was extended, my mom gave my dad the OK signal, and we all entered the home or gathering. But, it didn't always work that way.

I specifically remember a time we gathered with my mom's sisters and all the cousins at a pizza restaurant in Calexico. It was so much fun, and when the celebration came to a close, it felt way too soon for us kids. As we initiated the journey back across the border into Mexico, my mom decided that she wanted to take advantage of the light of day and go see one of her sisters. She had dad turn the car around and drive to my tia (aunt) Ella's apartment.

As usual, Dad stayed in the car while Mom and I knocked on the door. To our surprise, my nine-year-old cousin Martin was there and greeted us at the door. As the door opened wider, we saw that all of the sisters and cousins from the pizza place had gathered without us. My cousin's reaction said it all, *"Por que estan aqui?" ("Why have you come?").* He was only a child, so Mom handled it gracefully and said that she wanted to see the family. He did not live there and was visiting my aunt Ella, as was everyone else, though no one had mentioned any "after celebration" when we had been together earlier.

I immediately had a strong feeling of being unwelcome and unwanted and viewed my cousin as if he were the gatekeeper to the elite club indoors. It felt as if what they had was something we should want. Our uncle Jojo approached us and explained that they just didn't have enough room for all of us in their small two-bedroom apartment, so they didn't include us in the afterparty. Feeling sad and somewhat alienated, Mom and I returned to the car and told my dad what happened.

Normally, my dad was *(and still is)* a soft and submissive man who loved and catered to my mom. It was not often that he took charge when it came to matters of Mom's side of the family. However, in moments like those, when mom felt pushed aside by her own sisters, Dad stepped in as protector of my mom and all of us.

Upon hearing what happened, he made an executive decision that we were not going to participate in the drama, and he turned the car toward home. I could sense the heavy-hearted energy mom was carrying from being left out. I felt my dad's energy protecting her heart by stepping in as her knight in shining armor and taking her and us away from the unwelcoming place. This was one of the experiences that showed me that those we are closest to and love the deepest, are often the ones who hurt our hearts the most.

Fortunately, my mom had a knack of alchemizing situations. On our return drive, she turned the circumstances to our advantage and decided to shop for some out-of-country purchases before returning home. It was in moments like those with my parents that I learned not to remain stuck in hurt, anger, or self-pity.

At the end of the day, we returned to our kingdom unscathed. Our sanctuary in Mexico was large enough for all of us, and we had all the land and running space we needed.

We loved our life in Mexicali, though my younger brothers were born in Southern California, which my parents also loved. An immigration law had announced that parents who had children born in the United States could legally immigrate and seek permanent residency, so our family went back and forth between living in Mexico and staying in America with family.

My parents had been considering bringing us all across the border in a permanent move to the U.S., for an opportunity to show us a more abundant life. Knowing the process would be difficult, however, the idea was talked about in theory.

When it was brought up, I paid no attention, because it was all talk. Besides, I did not want to live anywhere else. I loved my friends and our family life in Mexico. I loved our home and the connection I had with the land, the rain, and the red dirt. I loved the feeling of being free to run with the neighborhood kids. Perhaps, I also didn't want to believe that it could happen, because I was afraid of having to leave everything that was known and familiar, and have to learn another language.

I wondered what it was about the U.S. that my parents wanted so badly anyway. We had everything we needed in Mexico, including our beautiful home with room to grow, great schools, a business that employed many of the people in our neighborhood, and several properties. Dad had always provided for all of us, including his mom and his brothers. He even provided a place to live for his late step-father until he died. To this day, my dad still helps his brothers in whatever way he can.

A few months after the incident with mom's family, on an afternoon that seemed like any other day, instead of dismissing us to go out to play after lunch, my parents sat us all down on the living room couches. They had upholstered them in fire engine red plastic, which they thought necessary to cover the original lime green furry plush material underneath. I think that was mostly to make sure the couches would not be ruined by our spills and sticky hands. As we sat for a family meeting, all I could think of was the sweat I felt between my legs and the slippery red plastic couches from the heat of the Mexicali summer, and my desperate desire to go outside and play.

I listened to the same presentation I had heard before about how wonderful America was, the benefits of living permanently in the United States, learning the English language, and being a preparation for a brighter future for us. The American Dream could be ours if we were willing to face the challenges.

In my eyes, there was nothing we could gain from permanent life in the U.S. I had heard the sales pitch before, but that day, their words had a different tone, a tone of declaration. As my thoughts swirled around everything we had and the impossibility of going anywhere else, I heard, *"Hijos nos vamos a vivir a Coachella." ("Children, we're going to move to Coachella.")*

My head catapulted around as my older brother, Manny, jumped with joy and elation. My younger broth-

ers, Nick, Rodrigo, and Jesse were too young to comprehend what was happening and had no reaction, other
than to watch Manny in his gleeful mania. They were not
in school yet, so they had no idea what any of it meant.
Nor would they have to undergo much of a change, other
than their home. I, on the other hand, sat in shock, disbelief, and devastation, *"I don't want to go."*

It was an announcement, however, a done deal,
non-negotiable. Moving to the U.S. was what they wanted
for us. And, we were going.

Looking back years later, I realized that what our
parents wanted most for us was a sense of belonging, to
make sure that no one would ever again open the door
to us and ask why we had come. They also wanted to
give us something internal, an experiential knowing of
another culture, new opportunities, another language
to communicate with, and expansion, so that we had
options and resources. What my parents couldn't have
anticipated was that the open-mindedness of American
culture would have a profound influence on me for the
rest of my life.

Chapter Insight - Going Deeper

Have you ever experienced something similar to my
reaction to my brother Manny's excitement, when you
noticed how different another's viewpoint was from your
own, and you immediately judged it as wrong or weird or
ridiculous?

My reaction to my brother was my inner judgment,
responding to my inner voice/storyteller that had already
created a belief in the story (meaning) about what the

move meant and what would happen. As a result of those two aspects influencing my behavior, I was resistant.

The inner judgment is the unconscious viewpoint that evaluates and then labels something as good or bad, right or wrong, smart or dumb, normal or weird, not enough or too much, rather than looking at the situation or person from a space of neutrality, the objective ease of the observer/higher self.

Can you recall, or realize, when the formation of your inner judgment appeared for the first time? What about the first time your inner voice told the story?

It happens without us noticing, because we've been conditioned, or habitualized, to automatically create and tell and judge the story. This automatic behavior is modeled for us by many influences over our entire lives, to the point that we are unaware of doing it. The engrainment is so deep and the attachment so strong that we actually identify ourselves by those inner voice and judgment aspects.

As we become increasingly identified with those two aspects, the observer/higher self that we were born with becomes muted, weaker, and less developed. And, the other aspects become stronger, more present, and more engaged with creating our experiences. Do you recall any situations that influenced your objective higher self to become quieter and the other aspects become louder?

During the drop by visit to my mom's sister's, I was influenced by seeing the judgment her family leveled on my family, though I wasn't conscious of it at the time. The voice/storyteller aspect in each of them collectively created a story they believed– *that our family was too big to invite, but they couldn't tell us that, because we would be angry or hurt*– so they didn't communicate with us at all.

My mom was directed more by her inner judgment and voice/storyteller viewpoints, to the point that she was held hostage by them. She was unaware/unconscious that she was not in control of her choices, behaviors, and emotions, which she could have been, had she not been so entrenched in the storytelling and reactive mode.

Sometimes, my dad's behaviors and decisions reminded her that there was another way to be. For the most part, my dad lived from a space of the neutral observer/higher self, except for those occasions when he was influenced by his protective side, to protect those he loved.

My parents' decision to return to our sanctuary after the experience with my mom's family was their way of showing me how to live from a place of neutrality and non-judgment. Did you have a parent or influence growing up who was able to be in this higher self aspect?

4

New Frontier - *La Frontera*

In choosing the things I would bring with me to our new home, I looked at what I needed to have and what I wanted to have. For whatever reason, I chose to leave a few of the gifts I had received, including a child's perfume in a bottle shaped like the shoe house from the story of the woman who lived in a shoe. I also left a silver comb and a mirror and brush set.

With most of our belongings packed, we were taking only what was absolutely needed. The rest of our clothing and possessions were piled in boxes and bags in disarray around us. We were leaving the house fully furnished and only taking clothes. Seeing that, I believed that our journey was a temporary one, like the others when we had left to stay with Mom's sisters and then returned. I left the things in my childhood room organized and in order for when I came back. I did not think for a moment that I would never come back to our home.

In retrospect, I can see that those temporary trips away from home were the inception of the pattern I had developed, thinking that the current "situation" was not really permanent or happening and that things would remain the same. I believed that those moments would last a lifetime, or happen exactly the same again. I found out later that those moments were unique and would never return. I would not have a second chance.

When my dad's large white van was not being used for his business deliveries, we all jumped in the back and rode on the floor for drives around town. At that time, there was no seatbelt law, and even if there had been, the van had no seats to attach seat belts to, except the front driver's seat and passenger seat, which was where Mom sat as co-pilot. When she rode with us, she always had something to say about how dad was driving.

Everything else in the van was open floor space, and with no seats or seat belts, nor a care in the world, we rolled around on the van floor to dad's sudden stops and wide turns. At other times, we used blankets or towels and pillows to create a sort of "tendido" (cozy resting space) to lay on the floor. During longer trips, we sometimes napped in the cozy blanket beds. If we drove the California coast and spent the night by the waves of the beach, the van became our family's mobile slumber party.

In moving to America, that summer of '85, the van became the vehicle we used to cross the border into the future of our lives.

We declared to the officer at the crossing that we were visiting family, as we had always said. Everything appeared to be as in our usual journey, until two hours later when we arrived at our final destination, Coachella California. Our parents had purchased new furnishings for the apartment we would call home. Mom had secured a position as the manager of the building, and dad had gotten a company construction job.

I felt the cool mornings of the Coachella Valley, just as I had felt the cool mornings in Mexicali. The routine of our days was as it had been in Mexico, except for one minor detail. We were in a different country. The reality set in after we were enrolled in school.

As a ten-year old child who could not speak or understand the language, I was assigned to the ESL (English as a Second Language) section of the classroom with all the Spanish speaking children on the first day of school. The English speaking students sat at the larger tables in the majority of the classroom to the right of us, and I sat with the ESL children at the smaller round table in a small section on the left.

Mrs. De La Torre was my ESL teacher, who assisted Mrs. Franklin, the lead teacher. We were taught similar lessons as the English speaking students, but in Spanish. We learned new vocabulary words to enhance our understanding and use of the English language. However, we couldn't play all the games, because we didn't have the words.

My days at school felt surreal. I was an outsider looking in the window, seeing our differences in the reflection of the way we dressed. We didn't wear assigned garments that showed our similarity, as we did in Mexico, which removed any need to compare anything except our physical features and aptitudes. In the U.S., all of the students styled themselves independently and wore brand names. I didn't understand the difference between name brand items and the items we liked from the discount retail stores we shopped at. Coming from a large family of immigrants, we didn't have the financial means to buy the things the other kids had. Our shoes and clothes separated us even more than our skin color and language, and I could sense it.

My family qualified for the lunch program, so I ate what others did who were from similar income brackets. At lunch, I knew who was like me, because we all ate the same foods. One day, a small cup of peanut butter was included in our meal. An English speaking boy in my class reached out to pick up my cup and asked me something. I didn't understand and quickly grabbed it away from him and pulled it close to my chest, staring at him. I didn't know how to communicate that it was not ok for him to take it, so I used my body language, and he twisted his face, mocking me. A classmate translated that he was only asking if I was going to eat it. Not understanding what was really happening made me feel even more self-conscious and separate from the others.

I had been afraid of learning a new language. What I didn't expect to discover, however, was that learning to speak and write another language was only a matter of developing a skill. More importantly, though it was not something I was aware of, learning a new language opened a door within me to a world where I could begin to develop the language of my soul. The new frontier was the Universe introducing me to various ways of communicating beyond my birth language, even beyond words.

That opportunity also ended up providing a space for me to be with myself when I was unable to express my feelings about what was happening to others around me, and when I was unable to express the lack of belonging I felt. It became clearer and clearer to me how challenging it was to share or express myself verbally, even physically, because I was made fun of. The feeling of being misunderstood– *or not quite understood*– and being obviously separate from the majority of the world began to imprint itself on me. This led to my desire to break away from my own body.

I was seeing who we, the family, were becoming, and who we no longer were. In wanting to create a sense of home, my parents did their best to build consistency in our new routine. Our life began to feel predictable. We began to spend more time with my mom's sisters and cousins, getting together weekly for Sunday Mass and spending the rest of the day together at a park or some-one's home.

In the evenings, though, instead of returning to our large hand built home in Mexico, we returned to the small apartment in Coachella. The entire space from the front door to the back wall of either of the rooms could be traversed in ten large paces. The children's room was made up of two sets of "literas" (twin bunk beds) for the five of us, and the other room was our parents'. With the seven of us sharing one bathroom, two bedrooms, and the living room, it was painfully small. And with no land for us to play on and no rose bushes for my mom to water nightly, we were like the perfume bottle that I had left behind, the woman who lived in a shoe.

It was at this time in the evenings when it set in that our life had changed, and that it was permanent. We were not returning. But, in the predictability that developed was a stability that allowed me to begin connecting with the new energy of the people surrounding me and the culture that we were assimilating.

One of those points of stability was the church down the street from the apartment that we walked past every morning on the way to school. It was said that the priest was anointed, that he smelled like roses, and that when he touched people's hands, the scent lingered on them. I missed the rose bushes of our home in Mexico, and I wondered if I would be able to smell the roses if I got close enough to him. But, I was only in fifth grade, so I didn't dare get close enough to find out. I didn't want to risk disrespecting the priest. Even if I did get close, I wouldn't have known what to say to him, and I didn't want to find out what would happen.

Still, I was curious to understand what anointed meant and how someone like a priest could have that direct level of connection to Spirit, God, the Universe. The priest was proof that a human could have a spiritual connection to God that had nothing to do with witch-craft, like the Bruja across the street, or the Brujo who healed the spell. God was showing me the Light side of a spiritual connection. I felt as if we were meant to live by that church, so I could see where Divinity resided.

The year after we arrived in the U.S., I developed skin cancer on my back. Being a devout follower of the church with the anointed rose-scented priest, my mom made a promise to the Virgin Mary. If God would heal me, my mom would go to Mexico to make an offering to the image of the Virgin of Guadalupe.

I honestly do not know how I got cured. My mom took me to a doctor, who removed the mole and the skin surrounding it. And that was it. I didn't have any other treatment. My mom believed that it was her prayer and her offering that healed me.

My mother didn't go to Mexico to fulfill her promise, because we were too poor. My parents didn't make enough money for all seven of us to go, and my mom was not going without my dad. But, she later pointed out the three birthmarks that formed a triangle on my upper right arm, like the three bright stars that shot out in different directions of the night sky on the night I was born. It served to remind me that surviving cancer and dodging death was another sign that something out there was overseeing that all turned out as planned.

Chapter Insight - Going Deeper

In preparing for our move to the States and looking around at all the boxes and furniture and possessions that were staying, I told myself– *the inner voice/storyteller*– that we were only leaving temporarily and would return. Can you relate to that? Can you remember the story of your experience and the inner voice telling it?

This inner voice that created the story that what I was hearing or seeing around me (the house in packed boxes and remaining furniture and possessions) was not really happening or real, and that would play a huge role in my experience years later.

Seeing the anointed priest expanded my belief and began to change the "story" that my inner voice talked about. That marked the opening of my point of view to see that connecting to Spirit went beyond spells and premonitions and brujas. Do you have an experience of a change in your spiritual beliefs or knowledge that changed the "story" in your mind?

The lunchtime peanut butter experience was an example of my inner voice/storyteller aspect (who was Spanish and did not speak or understand English) telling me that I was being taken advantage of, which my inner judgment aspect labeled as mean, wrong, and threatening.

Looking deeper, the judgmental and storyteller aspects of me feeling separate and mocked and not good enough were co-creators of my manifestation of skin cancer on my back. Experts like Louise Hay and Gabor Maté teach the mind-body connection between pain, disease, and other human conditions and unexpressed unconscious emotions and beliefs (stories). Having immigrated from Mexico, I was unable to speak the language and not a "real" American. I was out of place, segregated in the classrooms, and isolated with others who were different from the majority, like me. I was judging myself and telling the story that I wasn't good enough and nobody liked me. I couldn't express my words, abilities, or connection to others in the universe. I couldn't say, *"Don't touch my food."*

The fear of being mocked behind my back marked me, much like The Scarlet Letter. I was vulnerable and felt like I had a target on my back. In fact, the cancer resembled a target, a mole in the middle with a halo around it where the skin around it was changing. It was a target. This and another experience later in my life would lay the foundation for my interest and deeper dive into how this mind-body dynamic works.

5

Pantomime - *Pantomima*

In the Latino/Hispanic culture, a girl's fifteenth birthday is a special rite of passage, known as "quinceañera." My parents had always instilled in me the importance of arriving at this age as a virgin. Our Catholic upbringing celebrated a girl's fifteenth birthday as one of purity, and the community believed in this moral principle. So, it was typical for people to participate in the "chisme" (judgmental gossip) when a fifteen-year-old girl did not measure up to this standard.

In the traditional quinceañera ritual, the young woman wears a white dress to represent her purity. She is surrounded by friends and supported by the community in the announcement that she has reached this age of maturity with virtue. In her honor, the young women of her court dance a waltz with the young men. By the time I reached this milestone, I had come to embrace the American lifestyle, while still celebrating our Mexican traditions. Arriving at this day a virgin felt like a major milestone in my young life, like I was worthy of God's love.

What was simultaneously magical about this time was the discovery and power of my intuition. A week prior to my quinceañera, my dad picked me up after school and told me that Mom had something for me, and we needed to go see her. Immediately, my stomach filled with a surge of energy bubbling up from the center of my core. It radiated upward and outward to my extremities, and ended right below the crown at my forehead. In that instant, I knew that something good was coming.

When we arrived at my mom's worksite and I approached her, I noticed a small gift in her hands. As she handed it to me, the intensity of the feeling I had had before became very strong. I opened it to see a small gold ring with a pink stone, her gift to me to wear for my quinceañera. After seeing it, the energy in me subsided. This feeling became known to me as both the premonition of something good coming to me and the marking of when it had come to pass.

Those feelings continued to develop in my physical body over the years, and I became more and more attuned to my intuition, to predict when and how good things would happen. When the feeling began to bubble up in the pit of my stomach, the things that triggered it, or the events that were transpiring, attuned me to where the manifestation would come from. I started tuning in to the feelings I got in the messages connected to my body, I began to identify the language of the Universe, and the way Spirit was communicating with me.

I became aware of small signs, such as a telephone ringing that would then turn into a person calling to announce good news. I started to pay more attention to clues and signs like these. Sometimes, when someone mentioned an event or a location, my body immediately reacted and, shortly thereafter, I was invited to the event or the location of the event. It was quite a journey to notice the connections and confirmations of my intuition, which my body was picking up on, like an antenna and communicating to me. I began to feel assured of my ability to foretell future happenings, and my attunement developed and strengthened more and more throughout my high school years.

I also began noticing that when I touched people, my hands would land on the exact spot they had just been injured. It was as if an invisible message was guiding my hands, but I didn't know it or know why.

Although those new intuitive feelings were adding to my repertoire of abilities, I knew that I could not share them with others. Not only were they difficult to describe, but the capacity to foretell a situation was stronger than I was able to express in words. It was through the arts that I began to channel this energy within me.

High School became an interesting period of exploration of what felt good in my body. I joined the marching band's color guard flag team, took dance classes, and sang in the choir. As I acquired more expressive ways to move, I found myself interested in the performing arts, both as a form of self-expression, and as a method of survival. I discovered the protection of knowing that I didn't have to speak, as long as I could sing, dance, act, or be creatively fluid in twirling a flag around. All of these activities I engaged with, like dance movement and art expression, were safe alternatives for my body to express myself.

Joining a drama class and performing pantomimes immediately opened another outlet of communication for me. Stepping onto the stage to share the skit my partner and I created was freeing. We didn't have to use our voices at all and crafted an entire scene of slapstick comedy in which we made fun of objects that were not really there and tossed our bodies around. At one point in our performance, my partner attempted to take something away from me, and when I refused to relinquish it and dropped to the floor, she pretended to choke me.

My short, wildly curly hair bounced up and down off the floor, and my arms and legs flopped like loose electrical cords.

The roaring laughter of the audience fanned the fire of my self-expression, and I finally felt the crowd of my peers accepting me. They enjoyed our performance so much that, on the following day, they identified me as a real pantomime and invited me to express my emotions that way. I responded with exaggerated facial contortions and amplified body movements and didn't have to speak a word.

In being able to act out in front of the whole school without speaking, I learned more about myself. I felt free and able to be at a level of authentic self-expression I had never known before. As a teen, I took this as a message that it was safest to be vocally quiet and communicative only through art and movement. I discovered a reality where I could be noticed and accepted by others by using my body.

Although this became the most acceptable form of connection for me, it developed into a condition that came at a painfully high price. As my soul's voice became quieter and quieter, my body language grew louder and louder.

Learning about the power of my body and how it could get me noticed was new and felt good. My ability to communicate through touch and physical expression began to feel like a craving I needed to satisfy. I noticed that hugging friends, touching someone's hand, or being physically close to someone felt much better than speaking. Yet, I felt so lonely, because I could not communicate the thoughts inside my mind with my voice. And this inability widened the feeling of separation I had noticed as a child with my friend looking at the stars. Knowing how different I was from everyone had become the awareness that separated me more and more through the years.

Seeing that I had reached my quinceañera with "virtue," my parents trusted me with more freedom. At the same time, however, they also noticed my body developing and felt the need to protect me more. Their rules about overnights at friends' homes began to challenge my need for freedom. I actually considered going into the military, to get away from home, but my parents made it very clear that that was not going to happen.

My persistence and constant negotiating eventually wore them down. They acquiesced to my unrelenting grumbling about not being able to do anything, compared to my brother who had more freedom. I felt like I had won a level of independence and was finally given permission to have overnights and longer visits at my best friend's house. And, I took advantage of that permission all summer long.

Those months gave me the freedom to explore my femininity in ways I hadn't been able to before. I embraced my new connection to that part of me through physical touch and witnessing the beauty developing in my body. As I became more pronounced in extending touch and hugs and eliciting physical closeness with others, my ability to influence grew.

That summer also allowed me to bond with my best friend and her family, to the point of becoming part of their family. It was easier to develop more intimacy with them, because I felt more comfortable to show affection, something that did not come as naturally to me with my own family. I spent the majority of my time at their home with my friend and her brothers. Her older brother was

of drinking age, and the three of us sometimes experi-
mented with alcohol when their parents were away.

One afternoon, while hanging out with her brothers
and indulging in wine coolers, a situation occurred that
I had never experienced before. I felt an energy taking
over that was neither my mind, nor my higher awareness.
My head grew quiet and gave way to the desires of my
adolescent body. Nearly naked, I was touching and kissing
her younger brother, and my body moaned in response to
him pleasuring me.

My mind clearly said that this was not something a fifteen-year-old should be engaged in with her best friend's
thirteen-year-old brother. Yet, there I was, listening to
the sounds of pleasure my body was making. I knew
that I would not have crossed that boundary without the
influence of alcohol in my system. The influence of my
friend's brother and the alcohol in my system broke down
any healthy barrier that could have been established.

In the midst, I heard my best friend's voice of alarm
outside the bedroom and her knock on the door to check
in. And then, her older brother's voice stopped her and
told her to leave us alone.

Feeling shame and guilt, I heard my parents' judgment chastising me for participating in activities of
"debaucherous" nature and reminded me that love was
not given to women who were easy. My mother's voice
said, *"Quién te va a querer toda usada"* (*Who will want you
all used up?*) and my father's voice said, *"A quien le dan pan
que llore"* (*No one turns down an easy catch*).

The voices occupied one side of my awareness, and
the uncontrollable pleasure my body was feeling occupied the other. In dual consciousness, I was simultane-

ously aware of my physical experience and my mental processing.

After that experience and feeling the sensations and pleasure in my body, I questioned the purity I had held onto until my quinceañera. I second guessed all the things I was not "supposed to do," that I would be punished or sent to Hell. How could pleasure be punishable? A part of me wasn't so sure that everything they told me was really the right thing. I started looking around and realizing that no one was going to Hell. This was the beginning of me questioning the programming, the way I had been taught to live out of fear and shame and regret. I didn't see anybody else regret having fun, or drinking, or having sex.

Chapter Insight - Going Deeper

When I heard the voices of my mother and father in my head warn me about women who were easy or all used up, I recognized the inner voice/storytellers of this world. I also recognized the difference between those people and others who were more influenced by their observer/higher self aspect. I also began to notice when my voice/storyteller was taking over my observer/higher self.

Have you recognized when the inner voice/storyteller aspect of you is influenced by your inner judgment? It's when you start changing the story of what really happened to the story that you create.

Have you noticed when the observer/higher self is the higher, stronger influence?

When I became aware of small signs and clues and started to pay attention to them was when I began allowing my inner voice/storyteller to be influenced by my observer/higher self, instead of my inner judgment aspect. This was when I began allowing the higher self aspect of me to come out of the dormancy that my judgment had placed it in when I was seven years old.

How do you become aware of when your inner judgment is running your mind? Becoming attuned to the signs was vital for me, as it is for anyone who wants to learn how to move back into balance, allow healing, and feel peace. Most people aren't aware of how often they allow the inner judgment aspect to control their experience. This disconnects them from the natural harmonic frequency in their environments, and connects them with discordant energy of the people they're around and interact with.

This is why it's necessary to disconnect from the dissonant vibration of the daily activities in our lives. Technology, electricity, and even being in the same space as another person will influence your vibration, emotion, central nervous system, and the storyteller and judgment parts of yourself.

Drive without the radio on. Disconnect from social media. Disconnect from the phone. However, even being in the car without the radio can be discordant and depleting. Try this. After you've been driving for a bit, pull over and turn the car off. As you sit in it for a minute, you can still feel the dissonance of the car, which is affecting your vibration.

Take time to meditate, to be with your own essence, your own vibration, without the interference of other things, sounds, people. It's important to be that aware. Ground yourself. Take your shoes off and go find some earth to stand on to be grounded. You'll reconnect to the earth and the harmony that balances you within yourself.

Have you noticed small signs and synchronicities more? Do you recall when you first began noticing them? How does it feel in your body and spirit when you see signs and synchronicities?

When people are around each other for some time, their influences on each other become noticeable. They start speaking the same, dressing the same, thinking the same, doing the same things. This can feel positive, light, true, and loving. Or, it can feel heavy, uncomfortable, and judgmental. This is why it's necessary to be aware of when you start feeling out of harmony and ease. Who are you hanging around with, listening to, focusing on, learning from?

How do you feel when you're with someone who is inspired and compassionate and loving? Do you feel lighter, freer, and more in your heart center? There's a reason for this. All of those are the energy of flow, of being in the observer/higher self aspect. It is the aspect of heart-centered intimacy that connects us with all that is and opens us to receiving the help that God/Spirit/the Universe is always offering. If we're not in the higher self aspect, it's like we're on a different road, and there are no road signs.

The energy in an environment is what makes musical instruments, drums and strings in particular, begin to vibrate to the same frequency of the sound in the room. It's a natural occurrence, even if there is no sound detectable to the human ear. This is why, when the people in a group circle hum the word OM, they all eventually end up in the same tone or pitch.

Our bodies are our instruments of survival and thrival in our human existence. We attune ourselves to the vibration that surrounds us. Whether we are in a city, a small town, the forest, the beach, or the jungle, we attune ourselves to that environment, either intentionally and actively, or not.

When we want to connect to our heart-centered observer/higher self, we must connect to others who have developed a clear awareness of that aspect within themselves. These are the groups we can define as conscious communities.

Whereas the voice/storyteller aspect acts out things and speaks on things, the judgment aspect can control the way the storyteller speaks and acts. Toddlers learn to stay out of the street, because the adult or guardian told them they can't. However, around adolescent and teenage years, the person starts to test the programming authority, *"If I run fast and no cars are there, I can do it and be safe."*

When I found myself being intimate with my friend's brother and watching my adolescent body receive pleasure, it was my mind relinquishing control to my body. The voice/storyteller (my body) was acting out its desires without the judgmental influence. My judgment started to interject (questioning what I was doing and whether it was right), wanting to take control again. It was also wanting to make sense of what I had been taught was right and wrong and make an appropriate move from that discernment. But my body was in complete control, developing its strength and acting from the importance of the pleasure factor, even potentially confusing the pleasure as "love" and "loving intimacy." When the judgment voice is not in control, the body talker is in control.

Breaking from the influence of the judgment was what my observer/higher self was seeking, but it would not have sought it that way. It would not have engaged in disconnected intimacy with no regard for the love and respect I had for my best friend and her family. But, my observer/higher self was underdeveloped, so it could not take control in the way that it would have. As a result, my body acted out the desires through reaction.

6

My Burden - *Mi Culpa*

With the start of 1991, the hope of more temperate weather in the coming spring did not yet occupy our thoughts. By late February, the desert was cold, and most plants had become dry and yellow, dormant from the long cold nights. As crisp as the night air was, the contrasting warmth of the sun made the days less arduous. The seeds had been planted for the new year, and I was ready to experience their sprouting.

My best friend's family often had gatherings, and I was always included. To continue my experience of freedom, I made it a point to spend as much time as possible there. I felt that I had grown up so much since my quinceañera, mostly through embracing the maturity of my changing body, but also with the drunken experience at my best friend's house. I became curious about what it would feel like to have an intimate experience with a slightly older man. What I did not anticipate was that the universe would respond to my curiosity, and with speed.

At a weekend celebration where various family members gathered, I hung out with the teens in the backyard, waiting to be called in for the meal that the adults were preparing. My best friend told us that her cousin, Dennis, was joining us. I knew nothing about him, except that he was nineteen and visiting from North Carolina on his military leave. My piquing interest about him took over all other thoughts, and I grew anxious to meet him.

In the conversations with my friend's family, it became apparent that they wanted him to meet me. They wanted to see their cousin more often, and if he showed interest in me, he might visit more. They had grown to love me like their own and dropped hints of me becoming a permanent part of the family. I felt the same way about all of them.

When he finally appeared at the door, I was pleasantly surprised. He was tall and handsome, and seemingly kind. An instant connection formed between us, and my nervousness intensified at first, then eased when I felt his mutual interest. We played games with everyone, and by the end of the evening, were flirting with each other.

I kept looking for ways to get his attention, and by the end of the second day, we were inseparable. The family was pleased to see that we hit it off and interacted so well. In looking for more ways to make time to see each other, he started to teach me how to drive the car that he had rented. We made out of town visits to different family members, to give me opportunities to practice.

The days seemed longer than normal, because we were spending so much time together, exploring different scenarios of a future we could have. I felt that our connection was really good, and it made sense to me to create a long-term bond with him, to secure my place within the family.

Palm Springs was very much a sleepy town in those years, mostly centered around the hospitality industry and retired tourists who lived there part-time to escape the colder weather of the states they lived in. There was not much to do, other than be deviant and entertain ourselves in whatever ways we could create. We spent time planning games to play, taking long drives, cooking together, and watching adult movies. The weekends felt normal, with the only difference being that I got to pretend to be older. It was fun, even exotic, to have the freedom to be a teen with an older boyfriend, a military man who was not from around there.

The other characteristic about the desert was that it was a popular place for teens to lose their virginity. It was also common for the girls to fear potential pregnancy. I had been curious about what scenario would surround my loss of virginity. Part of my Catholic upbringing taught that we should wait until marriage. Yet, the internal conversation going on in me told the story that everyone my age was experimenting.

Everything moved very quickly with Dennis, and I found myself easily giving more of my attention and touch to him. The feelings running through my body when he touched me provoked me to wonder if they matched what I had seen portrayed in the movies. Getting closer to him and physically opening to more and more of his touch, seemed like a foreign progression that would lead to something greater than simply teens being teens. I was eager to spend the night away from home and explore the new secret romance we were developing.

My parents had no idea that I was seeing him, so there was no restriction or late-night curfew, or any awareness that there might be a risk in me staying at my best friend's. So, when I asked them if I could stay over one weekend, they said yes. I had no idea that there was any danger in spending the night at the home of the family I loved and had spent many overnights at. I did not realize that the practices I was engaging in– *exposing my body with my tiny booty shorts and tank top*– were attracting a kind of attention I did not want, the kind of attention I was not ready for.

On the second night of our weekend together, we settled in for a movie and homemade popcorn. The cold weather outside gave us an excuse to cuddle up with a blanket on the couches that my friend's parents had arranged facing the small living room television. We rented Jungle Fever, simply because it was rated R. We were pretending to be adult enough to watch the sexually, but violently charged adult movie.

We spent the majority of the movie holding hands, touching each other, and feeling the heat of our bodies under the blanket. I felt safe, because we were at my best friend's house, and her parents were in their room down the hall.

When the movie ended, everyone retreated to bed. Instead of bunking with my best friend, I decided to go with Dennis into the office that doubled as a guest bedroom. Holding his hand, I followed behind him into the room to a small twin-sized bed in the corner. I imagined that we would make out and then cuddle and go to sleep. As much as our closeness had progressed over the several days we spent together, I was not intending to go further than that.

We got into bed fully clothed, and I laid next to him, just as I imagined, cuddling. When he kissed me, I noticed that his breathing was becoming agitated. He got close enough to my body that I could feel his physical response to me. His hands moved all over my body, and I became alarmed that it might not be something I could slow, or stop if it came to that. As he continued, my mind started racing, thinking of what I could do to stall the progression. But, I could not scream, or I would wake my best friend's parents and be embarrassed from their knowing that I followed Dennis into the room. Guilt and shame took over again. I had made the wrong decision. I couldn't think fast enough on what to do to make the situation stop.

As he continued to do what he wanted, he kissed me and started to remove my pants. Not wanting to alarm him, I said, *"No,"* as timidly and non-offensively as I could. The weight of his entire body pressed me against the mattress. I said *"STOP,"* louder, but he put his hand over my mouth. Not believing what was happening, my mind said all the reasons that it would stop at any moment.

"Of course, this could not possibly be happening to me… Certainly, it had to stop, because I had said no… I had asked him to stop… Because he was my best friend's cousin, he would respect that… Because my best friend was right in the other room, he would surely stop… Because my best friend's parents were sleeping right down the hall, for sure he would stop, as I had asked."

But he didn't.

As the pressure of his penetration sent splintering pain into my virgin body, I felt myself separate into different directions. My body was on the bed gasping for breath at the bits of oxygen available in between thrusts, attempting to survive. My mind was clear across the room in the corner, managing the shock, powerlessness, sadness, disappointment, anger, shame and guilt. And another part of me hovered above my body, watching the entire act unfold, keeping the peace within me and maintaining the hope that I would survive now, and afterward.

When he finished, I leapt out of bed and felt the heat and fluid exiting my body between my legs. I looked at him, but he didn't attempt to hold me back, or say much of anything. I pulled on my pants. No other piece of clothing had come off. I walked out of the room and went straight to my best friend's bedroom to wake her.

Tears welled up from the feelings and the violation, and the voice in my head said, *"I was just raped."* Yet, I couldn't say it out loud, especially to my best friend. She was just a kid, like me. She wouldn't know how to react or know what to do. I didn't want to make her feel bad. All I could do was tell her what happened and watch her eyes fill with sadness. The only thing I wanted was to go home, but I didn't want to wake her parents, so I told her that I didn't want to wake them. Everyone's peace was more important.

I went into the bathroom to clean up the mess between my legs and smooth my hair, and then waited in her room and passed the time until daylight. I don't recall what I did. I was in a state of dissociation, going back and forth in my areas of awareness.

Something in my best friend's eyes told me that, although she believed me and had some compassion for what I had experienced, she also blamed me for what happened. She had seen how willingly I had connected with her cousin and the closeness we had cultivated, but she had also witnessed my allowance of the escalating touch and flirtation. Knowing my summer experience with her younger brother and watching me become more comfortable with the attention my body was receiving, she may even have thought that I invited it. Though she didn't utter any words of culpability to me, the look on her face was the judgment.

I loved her and could not bear the thought of disappointing her, so I took on what I believed to be her viewpoint, that it was all my fault.

When my dad arrived, I got in the car as though nothing had happened. I was quiet during the ride, grateful that my mom had not come. With my dad, I could feel safe. He wouldn't interrogate me about my visit. He always had a way of making life light and funny. And in that moment, I really needed light and funny.

When we got home, I went directly to my room and took a shower. Trying to avoid my mom as much as I could, I stayed in my room all day. Being so intuitive, she would know that something happened and ask me questions until I opened up and told her everything. Then, she would blame me and punish me. I was not supposed to have a boyfriend. My chances of ever going anywhere again would be ruined, along with my freedom and my parents' regard for me.

Chapter Insight - Going Deeper

The night I met Dennis marked the beginning of my awareness of how my thoughts had a direct connection to Spirit and the Universe to produce immediate results, whether in the form of an opportunity or an event. I started to see how my words and thoughts were coming to life, and how I was manifesting into reality the situations that I focused on. It was as my mom had shown me when I was a child. What she spoke became a reality, or a prediction of what would come to be.

Have you experienced this in your life, on a small or large scale, when you were wanting or thinking about something and then it happened?

This is how manifestation works. The observer/ higher self aspect of each of us has direct contact with the universe and the collective consciousness. When we are being present in this aspect, we are tapping into the collective consciousness. And when another person is in his/her higher self, this is when our angels talk with each other. Our higher selves are in constant connection with each other and with the energy of the universe, which is how things happen. This is manifestation. It happens all the time, but we aren't aware, and when we notice something, we call it a coincidence. However, like Albert Einstein said, *"Coincidence is God's way of remaining anonymous."*

While my heart wanted to connect with the man I had imagined creating a future life with, and my body enjoyed the closeness we were sharing, my internal chatter of guilt and shame supported the belief and the story I told myself that it was wrong. It was the dual consciousness again, when my inner voice/storyteller was being influenced by my inner judgmental aspect.

Have you ever been in the doorway to a possible situation where you were excited and felt a strong heart desire for something or someone, while at the same time, telling the story in your head why it wasn't good or right or possible? Or, have you felt a strong desire in your body or mind, but your heart or higher self was guiding you not to do it?

Looking back (in chapter 4), the pattern that developed in my childhood, of thinking that the current situation was not really happening (moving permanently) and believing that things would remain as they were, was a pivotal point in strengthening my storyteller aspect. That was the aspect that had the most influence and control during my rape. When I lay there in disbelief that what was happening was really happening, my voice kept saying that it would stop, so I believed it would stop. Even though I experienced a bit of guilt and shame, that inner judgment aspect was not as strong as the story and disbelief that it would go further, which is what allowed it to go further.

Have you ever been in a situation that was so outside your ability to believe or comprehend that you felt almost unable to move or leave the scene?

Unfortunately, it's very common for a woman who has been raped to not want to say the word "rape" and not view it as rape. This is partly because we disassociate. In my case, my disassociation was me identifying with three separate aspects of myself. My mind was managing all of the emotions and powerlessness, the judgmental aspect. My body was on the bed feeling the physical pain, telling the facts, the inner voice / storyteller. And, my spirit consciousness was overhead observing my body, while simultaneously maintaining peace and hope within me, the observer / higher self. I was all of them at once.

I had always been aware when the judgemental aspect of me was controlling the story that I was telling, or when the storyteller was controlling my body. In that moment, however, I was all three. Laying on the bed, I saw one in one corner of the room, another in my body on the bed, and another above me. It was so confusing that I disassociated.

A lot of people (boys and men included) say, *"This couldn't possibly happen to me,"* referring to rape or molestation. Then, when it does, we shame ourselves by thinking or saying that we caused it. I understood that it was rape. However, in facing my friend and seeing her accusatory look and feeling her energy of blame, while also judging myself, I took on her belief that it was actually my fault, that it was not rape at all.

In holding the belief that *"this couldn't possibly happen to me,"* and then having it happen, we can sometimes remain locked in judgment. And the inner voice/ storyteller then tells the story of what happened from the perspective of the judgment. Unfortunately, if the judgment aspect is so strong in its view of the situation that it cannot understand, love, forgive, or accept what happened, it will choose to view the event as either "too horrific to believe" or "unacceptable and shameful." And, then it may either completely block all recollection of the event, or change the details (story) of the event, in order to function and move forward.

This is true just as much for men and boys as it is for women and girls. I know a man who was raped at sixteen, but never owned it, never accepted it (faced the true story), until we were having a conversation forty years later. I said, *"You were raped."* He said, *"Yeah, I didn't know what to make of it."* The confusion and overwhelm comes from having so much judgment around something, that you can't believe it's real, or admit that it happened. There's nowhere to fit it in your belief and reality structure, so you don't do anything with it, except bury it away.

His recognition (seeing) that he had been violated opened the suppressed trauma that had been buried within him and allowed him to feel for the first time the emotions that he had blocked. For him this was a total breakdown/meltdown. He had to break down the walls of his story and let the emotions that had been trapped behind the walls melt all the way down. He hadn't owned it (faced and seen the true story) for all those years, so he could never release the hold (judgment) he had on himself. Once he did, the breakdown became the healing he had needed.

7

Self-Fulfilled Prophecy - *Profecía Autocumplida*

When I came clean with my parents, my mom became enraged that I had not told her when it happened and had hidden the relationship from the beginning. My chances for wearing white at my wedding, and being walked down the aisle, and feeling my father's pride were ruined.

As the months passed, my body healed. But, my mind recalled that February weekend with more shame and guilt than I could handle. My parents' words repeated over and over in my head like a broken record, *"Women like me are "mujeres facilitas" (easy women) and "usadas" (used goods). "Nadie me va a querer" (no one is going to want me).*

I decided that my parents were right. I was no good. No one would want me. I ruined my life and my body. I made bad choices and a mistake so big that I could not take it back.

Feeling lower than I had ever known, I yearned for acceptance, for people who might value me, and to connect to something that mattered. I took a job at the local movie theater that summer. I sought approval from an independent group of high school students. Most of the kids who worked at the movie theaters had free lifestyles, and their parents didn't monitor them as much as my parents did. This move into freedom led me to develop closer relationships with a few different crowds of people who had more life experience than I had.

Feeling that I didn't belong anymore, I distanced myself from the choir groups and the color-guard flag team, and marching band that I had auditioned for and earned my special place in. I disconnected from the "goody two-shoes" group of friends that I hung out in with my best friend. I no longer felt good enough to be part of any of them.

Earning money gave me a sense of freedom and a taste of what it felt like to grow up. It also gave me the independence to do things on my own and the ammunition to push boundaries at home. I continued asking for more freedom, more time away, and less responsibility for caring for my younger siblings. My parents bought a car for me, hoping that would motivate me to straighten out and, at the same time, enable me to come and go to work and school on my own. It may have been their way of making up for their own guilt, or to free themselves of the responsibility of one of their five children. Perhaps, they believed that I had shown a willingness to be more mature.

By the time the new school year started, I had immersed myself in the local party crew, called "Ladies of XTC." School wasn't really a priority for them, as much as skipping school to plan parties and underground gatherings with drinking, smoking, and other substances. The only knowledge I had of "ecstasy" was that it was an obscure feeling of euphoria, or a pleasurable sensation, neither of which I had experienced yet. I was clueless.

The majority of the girls in the group lived in the barrios of Palm Springs Dream Homes, an area my parents had intentionally kept our family out of. They had bought a home in Cathedral City to raise us in a nicer area. El Barrio Dream Homes was an older community of cold concrete and brick walled homes, unkept yards, and dilapidated structures. The streets were littered with debris, broken furniture, discarded appliances, and trash, among other things. The typical residents were working parents whose kids stayed out most days and returned home at sunset, or just before their guardians came home. As I created more friendships with the kids there and hung out at the neighborhood parties, the area became very familiar to me, like my second home. I felt like I belonged.

With a constant effort of persuasion, I was given more and more leeway by my parents. And, when they pushed back, I responded with disobedience and rebellion, which I also expressed in my appearance. I began dressing to match the other girls in the group and traded in my tight jeans and California sandals for baggy khakis and tennis shoes. To enhance my developing body, I wore padded bras and tight shirts. My make-up changed to thinly tweezed eyebrows, thick eyeliners that flared the corners of my eyes, and dark burgundy lipsticks that highlighted my thicker lips. The final change was making my long curly hair bigger, to further identify me with the "Cholas" of the town. I teased my hair and heightened my bangs, flared the sides and stiffened it all with lots of hairspray.

Being in the crew gave me a sense of importance and renewal, and I was welcomed as part of the family. By that point, I had become much more animated in my body and was given the nickname "TAZ," after the Looney Toons Tasmanian devil. My hair was wild. My energy was wild. And my actions were wild.

Prior to that year, I had applied myself and earned assignments to college level courses and medical assisting preparation. My senior year of high school was a blur. I spent most of my time starting and stopping projects and classes. I was the opposite of who I had been, a completely different person. The rape had spiraled me down to a place I had never been, without my awareness of how I arrived there. I knew that I was no longer the sweet girl who connected with the energy of angels and love and had a bright future. My trust in others and in myself had shifted. This, in turn, created a barrier that prevented others from entering. As much as it was a shield to protect me from the bad, the barrier was also a block against the good.

However, even the shield was not enough to protect me from the influence of relationships and environments that catalyzed a continual spiral downward over my next few years. I involved myself with the head of one of the party groups, the "P-Tribe." "P" stood for "Perros" (dogs). These single guys were not interested in relationships. Their parents worked long hours, so they had little to no supervision and too much free time. They focused on creating parties that brewed chaos, including fights, and the occasional shotgun fire.

Knowing that he lived in the Barrio Dream Homes, I was flirting with disaster. But, the fact that he came from a large family and parent immigrants like me and my parents, was familiar. The glimpse of his leadership was probably what drew me to him the most and instantly attracted me. The part of me that wished so much to feel worthy of something good, or someone good was alive and running me. My self-image had been broken. I felt used and, like my parents said, no good. Identifying with that group fed my lack of self-worth. Feeling seen and included in a community was what I needed more than anything. I tried to find some worthiness and a sense of meaning in something, or someone. Above anything else, I had a craving to be accepted, and that the head of the P-Tribe wanted to spend time with me was the fulfillment of my craving.

I allowed our connection to develop into a romantic relationship. I was then a partner. I had someone who valued me, wanted me. Surprisingly, my parents were supportive at first. Eventually, though, they were opposed to me staying out late and going out with him, even to visit his family, because they lived in the Barrio. Their refusal to my continual requests for permission to see him and go to parties became too inhibitive, and their restrictions only lit the flame of my rebellion. The more they declined, the more they fanned the fire within me to be emancipated and free. In my eyes, I had nothing to gain or offer anyone while under my parents' thumb.

To be in partnership with someone who valued me was enough to motivate me to take a risk I would never have considered a year earlier. At seventeen, I dropped out of school and ran away to live with my boyfriend. We lived with his parents the first couple of months and then moved into an apartment with some others.

Less than a year later, I was pregnant with my first child.

Chapter Insight - Going Deeper

Looking back on the summer before my last year of high school, I see the beginning of my self-sabotage. It may have begun that day with my best friend's younger brother. But the rape by her older cousin was the tipping point that precipitated everything my parents had wanted to protect me from. I had almost completed high school, with high grades, a good foundation, and a supportive family, and suddenly took a detour. I dropped out of school, moved to the exact neighborhood my parents tried to keep us away from, got involved with the kind of person they tried to protect me from, and became a pregnant teen.

My parents' opposition to me going out with my boyfriend from the Barrio, even to visit his family, was both my mother's judgment aspect and my father's protective state, which came from judgment of the story he and my mom shared about people from the Barrio.

Can you relate to having a parent or someone you knew who operated mostly from that controlling judgment point of view and the story they believed?

Deciding later that my parents were right– *that no one would want me because I was no good and ruined my life and my body and made a mistake so big that I couldn't take it back*– was my inner judgment viewpoint overpowering both my storyteller (believing a story that wasn't true) and my observer/higher self. And because the judgment was that strong, it influenced me enough to create a reality that looked exactly like the story my parents had warned me about and tried to keep me from. This is the way self-sabotage works.

As I think about the things my mom had predictions about and the announcements my dad made, I realize that I did all of them. Unconsciously, I fulfilled every prophecy they warned me about. My parent's worst nightmares had become my life, and theirs. My realizations were confirmation that our thoughts and words create our reality.

8

Why the Caged Bird Sings
Por qué Canta el Pájaro Enjaulado

After finding out that I was pregnant, my parents let me move back home, while reminding me that I had failed again. They tried to guide me back from the abyss I had fallen into, with a baby in my womb and a boyfriend by my side. On the contrary, however, in my perspective, the father of my baby was a good man. He was a leader who didn't back down from his responsibility, someone who was willing to stand by me. As we tried to become parents, while also grow into adults, my parents gradually grew to trust my partner as a man worthy of their support.

However, in order to live at home with my boyfriend and earn my parents' trust again, he and I were required to finish high school. I re-enrolled in homeschool and turned in all my work on time, which barely allowed me to qualify, and my boyfriend went back to finish high school.

I wanted to go away to college, but after running away and getting pregnant, my parents were not going to let that happen. The only way I was going to be able to leave their home was if I married my boyfriend. Being married to the father of my first born was what was needed, for their comfort, and for the sake of appearances.

Our daughter was born on March 16th. Seeing my mother in the birthing room with us and her love for me and my new baby, despite all the trouble I had caused, gave me a glimpse of what unconditional love was. I finally understood what she had gone through delivering five children.

And, I witnessed it again watching my parents take care of my daughter and seeing my father's commitment to helping me care for her. He became the happiest and proudest grandpa of his little pride and joy, and brought her to me to breastfeed every day at my lunch hour at the retail store I worked at. He loved his granddaughter and nurtured her as if she were the most precious being to ever exist. What I saw in him was pride that his legacy was growing and our family's next generation was beginning. His commitment to care for her and me was a deeper demonstration of unconditional love than I had ever experienced, or witnessed. Until I became a parent and saw my parents being both parents and grandparents, I did not have the capacity to observe unconditional love.

Having a child was a turning point for my husband and me. We realized that we weren't playing games anymore and that we could not have the social life that we had before. We needed to become parents. With that understanding, we somehow built a life together.

What had seemed a mistake, or a failure, running away and becoming pregnant turned into a big, bright bow-tied blessing. Giving birth moved me into a space of purpose, a reason to live. I had motivation to succeed and a desire to do my best, so that I could be a positive role model for my daughter.

During breastfeeding time, I had conversations with her, and we bonded and played. I promised to tell her that I loved her as much as possible, to protect her, and to teach her about life. I promised to give her the things my parents couldn't give me. She was the miracle I needed to turn my life into something worth living.

This opening of my heart and awareness was what I needed to make the commitment to her father. On April 16th, one month after our daughter was born, I married her father.

The next few years felt light and bright. My husband and I entered college. We bought a house near my parents. I reconnected with my creative side. College refreshed my ability to see possibilities, and I stepped into a career as a counselor. I also became the lead singer for a band. I was an adult with full support from my parents and brothers, and life was looking up. Constantly exposed to new experiences that awakened my curiosity and zest for life, only good was coming on the path that I was walking.

The women counselors I worked with had had children when they were young, like I did. We had similar backgrounds, all marrying young, and all taking the opportunity to work in a career where we could help people overcome barriers in their lives. I believed that we were qualified, not just because we were capable of doing the technical work, but also because we had overcome barriers in our lives and landed on our feet. We became like sisters, and as our friendships developed, we started to have fun going out at night with our husbands.

Yet, with all of that, I gradually found myself feeling unfulfilled. I had no idea what was missing, but I was searching for something that my life didn't have. To quell the restlessness, I started seeing a therapist, who then referred me to a psychiatrist, who prescribed Prozac and Xanax. My overactive mind quieted, but the drugs made me numb. I became unable to feel the connection with people around me, including my husband and my daughter.

I wanted that connection back. I wanted that feeling of aliveness, some indication that something was living within me. Eventually, stuck somewhere between aliveness and death, I became emotionally removed from my sense of self, and from my life. College was no longer motivating and inspiring to me. Even the friendships with my sister counselor friends offered no relief from the numbness. The effort of it all was only exhausting me, as if I were living the life of an older woman who had a pile of responsibilities. My energy didn't fit my age and life experience. I looked for the light at the end of the tunnel. But it wasn't there.

Still, I continued to socialize with my co-worker friends. It evolved into a weekly routine of experiencing the latest trends in the desert nightlife without our husbands. The first was salsa dance classes. We felt the fire and freedom in our bodies as they moved with the music. The freedom tempted us to go beyond the classes, and we started to go dancing at the nightclubs. Dressing more and more provocatively, we stayed out later and later. Our husbands became our babysitters, while we lived the other side of our dual lives.

It was there that I found the aliveness I was looking for – *the high that dancing created in me and the emotional connection of the many creatives surrounding me.* It was like what I had in high school. I found aliveness in the independence I experienced, flirting with others who came dressed to impress, getting lost in the music and the alcohol, and allowing my spirit to move my body. Most of all, I felt alive singing with my Tex-Mex band

and receiving the admiration of the people watching, like the pantomime experience.

Returning home, after expressing my energy so freely on those nights, became boring. That craving for constant aliveness distracted me from my studies. I wanted to focus on the creative side of dancing, guitar and piano lessons, and singing. Work was no longer satisfying and purposeful, only a release from my life as a parent, wife, and counselor. I found myself looking to free myself once again from entrapment. But, no one was holding me captive. I had chosen my own cage. I had created it and put myself in it.

The weekends became quick escapes, as I began to find ways to spend more time out on my own. I devised excuses to tell my husband and my parents that allowed me to exercise my freedom. At first, it was joining study groups for college, getting to know people, and simple activities to justify going out after school or work and staying out on weekends.

At the peak of my deception and disconnection from my personal ethics, I was no longer listening to what was right or wrong in the mental discipline that had previously kept me from going off the rails. I surpassed the point of deceiving myself and pretending that what I was doing was justified and harmless.

The momentum increased to the point that my excuses created a life of their own, and I decided to push the limit of my husband's kindness. One Friday evening, I left Palm Springs with my friend, her lover, and my dance teacher. We drove to Los Angeles, where the night clubs were bigger and the dancers were more fun.

With a ton of guilt, I returned home two days later. My husband's car was gone. I called my parents and my in-laws, but my daughter was not with any of them. Our families were the only people we ever left our daughter with, so I knew he wasn't at work. I contacted all the people we knew, but no one seemed to know where they had gone.

My parents had only words of blame toward me. My mom was very clear that if anything happened to my daughter, it would be my fault. I knew what I had done. I had lied and left my family, to have fun, to feel free, to pretend that I was not married, not a mom, not a bird in a cage.

After receiving confirmation from everyone that they had not seen my husband and daughter, I finally went to his work and found him. He had never left her with anyone who was not family. I asked where she was, but he refused to tell me and warned me to not even think about going home. But, I needed to make sure that my daughter was safe and taken care of. I could never forgive myself if I had placed her in harm's way. I told him that I wouldn't leave his sight until I knew where my daughter was.

I wanted to make things right, but I felt lost and crazy. My fear and helplessness triggered memories of the rape and the powerlessness I felt at the hands of a man who I believed cared for me. I thought of my own daughter being hurt and alone and helpless. Spinning out of control, I made a scene, until his manager came outside and asked me to leave. He warned me that I would be removed from the premises if I didn't.

Unable to face anyone, I left his job site and went back to our home. Wanting to see if any clues were left that could help me find my daughter, I pulled into the garage and went to the front door. I turned the key in the lock, but it wouldn't open. All the window blinds were closed. I went around the side of the house to climb in the window, but he had secured all of the windows closed with new metal locks.

Feeling more and more powerless, I went to the garage. Fueled by the energy of rage and anguish, I pried open the door and lifted it. Walking through the darkness of our empty home, I saw that he had blocked the front door by wedging a chair under the knob. He had also removed all the telephones from the wall connectors, so I couldn't call anyone. I saw that all of my daughter's things were intact. He hadn't taken anything more than an overnight bag. Filled with relief, I thought, *"They're coming back."*

I took a bath and cleaned myself up, so that I could have a clear space to think. I pulled out my journal that I had been writing in since I was nineteen. It was my space to have deeper conversations with myself, and with God. I wrote and wrote, surrendering my secrets, my emotions, and my mistakes, the bad decisions, missteps, and pain. It was all my fault. Everything. I blamed myself.

I waited, and I wrote. As the minutes turned into hours, and the night grew later and later, my frustration created such dissonance in my nervous system that I was beyond control. I reached for some pills to calm my nerves, but they did not ease my emotions. My parents' words circled in my mind, *"Si algo le pasa a la niña va a ser tu culpa,"* (*"If anything happens to your little girl, it will be your fault."*).

I took a few more pills and continued writing. With each additional pill, my mind faded. The journal entries shifted from reflections and repentance to a goodbye letter to my husband and my daughter. As I wrote the last word, I grabbed the bottle of pills and took more.

My husband and my daughter came home. We argued, and I told him that I had taken some pills. He didn't care and said, *"Good. You should've finished them."* So, I grabbed the bottle and took the rest. Then, I picked my daughter up and carried her into her bedroom with me and locked the door. I held her in my arms, fading in and out of consciousness.

Chapter Insight - Going Deeper

Becoming a parent and seeing my parents love and care for my child was the first time I got to observe (observer/higher self) unconditional love from my parents. That is the heart-centered intimacy of the higher self. In seeing that, I was able to view my situation from the non-judgmental higher self viewpoint of the blessing. My experience of seeing that and feeling the heart-centered intimacy for my child opened me to realizing that I had a purpose, a reason to live.

Yet, I was still under the oppression of the rules and suppression of the judgments of my parents, culture, and community "chisme" ("gossip"). I felt trapped, like a bird in a cage, not free to be the flying bird that I was and spread my wings. Under the weight of oppression and suppression in the judgment and stories of our life is a voice that longs to be heard.

Have you ever felt that way?

Do you know anyone who attempted suicide, or thought about it, whether or not it was premeditated? That thought or decision is the outcome of the judgment overpowering the storyteller, creating a story that is not true. And, have you ever tried to talk with the person, or seen someone try to talk with the person, like in a movie? The person is so controlled by the judgment and storyteller aspects that he/she believes the story is true. At that point, I believed the story, which was: I had nothing to lose. And I succumbed to that belief.

9

Two Steps Forward - *Dos Pasos Adelante*

As destiny arranged it, my mom had an intuition and asked my dad and brother to make an unexpected visit late that Sunday night. Knowing that I didn't know where my daughter was, my mom wanted to drive by to see if there was any new finding. When they saw my husband's car outside, and not mine, they stopped.

My husband told them that I had taken some pills and locked my daughter and myself in her bedroom. My mother rushed to call the paramedics, but found all of our telephones taken out of the wall connectors. So, my brother ran out of the house and down the street as fast as he could to find the nearest gas station with a public phone.

In a moment of awareness, I heard the paramedics knocking at the bedroom door and looked down at my daughter. I don't remember how, but I stood up and opened the door. My daughter went to my mom as the paramedics put me onto a gurney and into the ambulance to try to resuscitate me. Somewhere between the living and the dead is a place called oblivion, where you have a body, but you're not fully in it. I felt the paddles on my chest, then a rush of the air being pushed into my lungs.

I woke up on the hospital bed in ICU, with my eyelids shut tight and a feeling of something lodged in my throat that would not let me breathe. I tried to inhale more forcefully, more deeply, but my throat was too tight and obstructed. In between breaths, I felt my chest being pushed up and down, as if it were a machine. My arms were heavy, but I managed to raise them up toward my mouth and touched the rigid object that was stuck in my throat and gagging me. I pulled on it with all my strength, but it wouldn't come out. With all my might, I tried again, but it caused a shooting pain down into my chest.

Imagining that I could time my pulling with the rhythm of the machine that controlled my breathing, I tried again. With every few seconds, each time the pressure subsided, I pulled the plug a little, then a little more, and a little more until, with one final deflation and pull, I pulled it all the way out. I could breathe.

I heard a loud beep, followed by a long, constant, high-pitched alarm. I didn't care. But, my head felt hazy, so I turned to my side. The relief was so calming that I fell into what seemed like a deep sleep. But I was quickly interrupted by a woman's voice, *"Oh sweetheart, what did you do to yourself?"* She turned the machine off.

They told me that my stomach had been pumped from a deadly dose of pills, and I had been in ICU for more than three days. If my mother had not followed her feeling, and had my brother not run down the street to the gas station on Maravilla and Ramon Road, I would not have been lying in that hospital bed.

My unconscious move to leave my body had not succeeded. I had been given another chance to live.

There was a purpose for my life that had been confirmed the night I was born, as my mother witnessed in the night sky. Written in the birthmark on my arm, I was meant to bring something to life, to fulfill an assignment. And, my mother's nudge to come to the house and find me was another reminder that she had not yet fulfilled her promise.

In the years that followed my near death, I returned to my job as a counselor. My husband and I sought therapy for our marriage until we reached a point when we were ready to give it another chance. Shortly after that, I gave birth to our second child. He brought so much joy to our lives with gurgling sounds that I had only heard in dolls or movies.

While I was beside myself in love with him, I was also deep in postpartum blues. Locking myself in our apartment for days, I didn't answer the phone or the door. Even food did not entice me, which made me extremely sad. I ate peanuts and sat on the couch with my son for days, until I noticed one day in the dimly lit room that his skin was a different color than mine, and slightly yellow. I opened the blinds, and went outside to sit on our patio. Within a few days of doing that, the nurturing light of the sun brought back his pink skin tone, as well as mine.

That was the impetus that shook me out of my rabbit hole. For the sake of my son, I couldn't stay locked up indoors. His skin spoke me back to reality, to life, to the outside world. Joy came back in, and I felt secure that I could make my life work. I did everything I knew to restore my mental strength and be the best wife, mom, student, and counselor I could be. I had a career. I had friends. I had a great family.

When the day came to return to work, I dropped off my daughter at school and brought my son to his babysitter for the first time. As I walked out the door, I felt the emotions rise and the tears well up. I gave up trying to hold them back and cried all the way to work, counting the minutes until lunch, when I could go see my baby and breastfeed him. The emotional tug went on for over a month, until at seven months, he no longer wanted to breastfeed, and I stopped leaving at lunch to see him.

My life was in a new routine, being a mother of two, going to school, going to work, and enjoying a healthy social life. I even took a role in a comedy performance group at work. In a creative space, I was contributing to a positive work environment and thriving in every area, so I thought.

One morning, as I pulled up my hair to put on the wig for a performance at work, one of the women in the group pointed to a lump at my neck and told me that I should have it checked. She had been diagnosed with lupus and recognized the sign of lymph node swelling. I dismissed her suggestion. Several weeks later, it became quite noticeable, and she really encouraged me to go to the doctor. Reluctantly, I made an appointment.

Dr. Lipfschutz, an endocrinologist, ran several tests, all of which came back normal. Before continuing with what he thought might be the final test, he asked me a kind of question I had never heard, *"What is it that you are not saying?"*

I didn't understand and asked him to repeat the question. He looked straight into my eyes and described what a chakra was. Then, he said that my throat chakra was being affected. Still having no idea what he was talking about, I asked, *"Chakra what?"* He explained that emotions have the potential to cause illnesses in the body. Emotions about not being able to express myself were affecting my throat chakra.

His words compelled me to look back at all the times I had held in my thoughts and emotions. I recalled when I sang Mariachi and when I sang in a choir and how I want-ed a singing career. I thought about when I was a lead singer in a band and when I sang and acted out paradies in a comedy group. None of them led anywhere, but I had always wished they would. I thought back on the numerous times my mom had told me how confused or delusional I was. She thought my ideas and desires, even my premonitions, were far-fetched. Wanting to do something big with my life, including my desire to become a singer, was too foolish to take seriously.

I saw the times I was unable to express what I really felt and thought. I considered my inability to make decisions for myself, including whether or not I wanted to get married, or enlist in the military, or attend college, or have sex at the age of sixteen, or say no. I thought about all the times I wanted to express my true self freely, but didn't share what I heard, saw, or felt, out of fear of being mocked or judged or shunned. I thought of how I couldn't share what came from my connection to spirit guides.

I continued thinking about this, until weeks later when I sat waiting for the biopsy result at John F. Kennedy Hospital in Indio, California. It was the hospital I had delivered my daughter at so many years prior. My mom and I sat in the room, grateful that everything had gone well. As I was being released and getting ready to leave, Dr. Lipfschutz came into the room and asked my mom and me to sit down. He explained that he was releasing me with the intent to allow my body to rest and heal a few days before returning for a series of extensive procedures to remove a tumor. I had throat cancer. Like an alien invasion, the tumor had attached itself to my carotid artery and was aggressively moving toward my brain and my heart.

Having cancer show up in my throat affecting my ability to speak suddenly made sense. It was a physical manifestation, an outcome of a long period of emotional suppression, limitation, and judgment by myself and others.

It all felt surreal, far removed from my reality. I turned to see my mom's eyes well up in the same uncontrollable way mine had when I left my son that first day at the babysitter's. I saw that pain in my mom's eyes one time before, when I was in labor in that same hospital, giving birth to my first child. All of that was in my mother's eyes. But there was more. I recognized those emotions that came from the realization that we parents cannot take away the conditions our children experience, or protect them from harm, or remove their suffering.

What I saw was fear. I had cancer again. My mother was hurled back seventeen years when she promised to see the Virgin de Guadalupe if my life could be saved.

Chapter Insight - Going Deeper

In the minutes that I was swallowing more pills, succumbing to the judgment and story that I had nothing left to lose, my mom was tuned in to her higher self connection and receiving the message to drive to our house. This part of ourselves is always connected to the collective consciousness, the higher selves and angels of all humans. They are communicating with each other all the time and sending messages to us to guide us. But, most people aren't used to connecting with their higher selves, so they don't get the intuitions. Or, they don't pay attention to them. When we are like my mom, we get the messages, and we trust them to be true. My mother's intuition was her connection to Source.

Have you ever had an accident or other experience, which had the effect of shifting you into that in between place, between consciousness and being out of body? When I was in the ambulance, in my body only enough to feel the paddles on my chest and the air being pushed into my lungs, I was no longer existing in my storyteller or judgment aspects. I was in the state of the neutral observer/higher self, witnessing myself in the scene.

In surviving the overdose and having my second child, dying was no longer my choice. Then, when I was diagnosed with throat cancer, it was as if the Universe was saying, *"I thought you wanted to die, so here. We're giving you what you want."* And I was saying, *"Wait. No. I'm trying to live now."*

Looking back on my life, I had experienced so many situations of my voice being silenced. I had opportunities to speak, but was met with the judgment, *"No, that's unacceptable. You should not speak. Don't say that. You don't know what you're talking about..."* I couldn't even call what had happened to me for what it was, "rape." I was so influenced by the judgment and storyteller that I was not able to express myself.

And, from an energetic perspective, the piece of the machine that was lodged in my throat was like the forces that had kept me from expressing myself, words being caught in my throat. Ultimately my unexpressed truth and stuck emotions accumulated in my throat and neck to the level of toxicity that it manifested into cancer.

PART TWO

PATH TO HEALING

CAMINO A LA CURACIÓN

My entire life has been a continuous series of invitations to discover my worth and my truth and, therefore, be able to see others' worth and truth. From that viewpoint, I continue my story now, by sharing how I uncovered the observer/higher self in me, after realizing that the inner judgment and voice/storyteller had been controlling my entire life without my knowing.

10

On Purpose - *A Propósito*

If I was going to die, I wanted to have fun before I did. I wanted to die happy, doing the things I wanted to do, all the things I had not been allowed to do my whole life, because they were "sinful" or bad. I had lived in the way others and I had judged right and good, and the way that my parents had wanted, in fact conditioned, me to live. They had wanted me to go to school and then get married, because I had messed up and had a child. In living under all the expectations, rules, and judgments I was raised with, I had never had freedom from judgment, or any control over my life. I didn't ever use my voice– *which is why I lost my voice.*

I wondered if doing all the things I wasn't supposed to do might actually make me happy, because doing what I was supposed to do had definitely not made my life easy or happy. I had followed the rules. And, I was dying. In a way, I felt grateful for the possibility that I might die, rather than have to continue to live in a world filled with rules and constructs made up by people with such limiting paradigms. I needed to live my last months, or years, without attachment to any of the rules. I needed to own my voice.

Not knowing what would make me happy, but daring to try it all, even the taboos, I spent the better part of my battle with cancer in a reckless state of freedom. The next few years felt like a rollercoaster ride, on which every turn was a free fall, a belly drop, or a throat lump. My vocal cords got damaged from the surgeries. I had not only lost my energetic voice to express myself, but after the surgeries, my physical voice was gone too.

When you decide that you have nothing left to lose, life looks very different.

When you have nothing to lose, you don't stay in captivity for long.

College degrees don't matter.

Life is no longer dragged out by retirement plans.

Traveling anywhere on a whim is the norm.

Staying in a broken marriage isn't important, no matter how many times you've tried to rebuild it.

Breaking a heart in betrayal forms a callus that hardens.

Money and stability are no longer a thing.

Living from the trunk of your car makes sense.

When you have nothing to lose, exploring risky alternatives is enchanting.

Coming home is no longer familiar, because nowhere is home.

Being a parent is put on pause and passed to more capable hands and hearts.

Permission to be reckless is a given.

Gender, love, and sexuality are undefined and limitless.

Being in a relationship with a stripper is a fun adventure.

When you have nothing to lose, no behavior is forbidden.

Being the only sober one in a field of drugs at a rave is natural.

Being the only girl in the Mandalay Bay Club top floor penthouse in a group of men with white powder is just another experience.

Getting lost with strangers when no one knows your location is risk-free.

Heaven and Hell are no longer scary, because they're the same.

There is no mystery to the outcome, because the outcome is always the end.

When you have nothing to lose, you look in the mirror and find that YOU are the only thing left to lose.

You don't fear rock bottom. You've been there, and the only way to go from there is up.

The ride was unpredictable, scary, and confusing, as I was both the passenger and the operator. It was all up to me. And none of it was up to me. I had nothing to lose, which was a much needed blessing. In my desire to own my individuality, voice, and sovereignty– *mistakes and all–* I lived without fear of death.

My cancer diagnosis was not merely a life-threatening death sentence and destabilizing disease. It was a permission slip to live in a state of complete freedom from restrictions, judgment, and fear. It was a paradigm shift meant to throw me off so completely that I broke the programming of the person I had become.

And, in breaking the mold of who I had been, I ended up rising from the ashes. I was declared cancer-free.

"Wait. What? I'm going to live?"

"I'm not going to be struck by lightning for not attending mass every Sunday?"

"I won't be damned to Hell for not wanting to be married to the father of my children?"

"I won't be excommunicated for spreading my wings and living away from my family?"

"I'm not going to be punished for sharing custody of my children, instead of being the primary parent?"

"I'm not exiled from my chance of happiness because I broke the rules of the Catholic church?"

In awe of discovering that all the things I was taught were the "norm" were suddenly options that I could decide not to choose, I became angry– *not angry at life–* *angry at the programming.* I looked at all the rules and taboos and teachings that I had been raised with, that I had agreed to believe about what was right and wrong and good and bad and acceptable and unacceptable. It was all nonsense. None of the constructs about proper conduct were real. They were all made up.

I had had cancer twice. I had almost died from an overdose. I had spent all my life following the rules, and I was never truly and completely happy. I said, *"YOU are wrong. I will not give you the keys to my happiness. From now on, I will make my own decision. Thank you, but no thank you."*

When I shifted into an energy of righteous rebelling at the conditioning, and surrendered to embracing the permission I had "earned" to do anything and everything I wanted, I fell into a state of true ease within my being. And, in that place, my state of dis-ease ended. I did not dic. I had triumphed at the Big C. I was alive, and I was ready to thrive.

With my new lease on life and my chance to live fully expressed, it was clear to me that I was being given the opportunity to re-know myself as a human. And I was taking that opportunity, with the additional awareness of all the blessings in my life.

I wanted to create stability around the free person I was becoming. I wanted a new space, with a new identity, and a new connection to myself and Spirit. I was ready to align with a purpose-driven path, choosing on purpose, living on purpose, finding my purpose.

Running the choices I made over the next few years was the drive to prove that I was good enough, good enough to be accepted, good enough to be valued, and good enough to live the way I wanted to live.

However, in the beginning of creating a life that made me happy, I wasn't exactly sure what that was. So, I took it a step at a time, changing one thing after another, moving forward in the direction of a life worth living.

In 2002, I filed for divorce and received fifty-fifty custody of my children.

With that came a desire to get out of the desert. The Palm Springs community I had been in suddenly felt too confining. I needed to be outside the small pool of my parents, my husband's family, and everyone who knew the person I had been and the things I had done. I was growing out of that person, and I needed to be as far away from the limitations of that as possible. I wanted to experience more aliveness, more fun, and more freedom. I moved to Orange County, California.

In living farther away, however, I wasn't able to see my kids as often as I had. So, I went back to court and was granted a better custody arrangement and schedule. These improvements allowed me to begin to live the life I had always wanted.

I went back to school at a faith based university to complete my undergrad program. Over the next few years, I lived by myself, attended school full time, worked full time, and spent time loving my children.

In 2006, I earned my bachelor's degree in Human Development, with an emphasis in counseling and graduated cum laude. My focus inspired curiosity about the psychology of people and the creation of our thoughts.

That same year, just prior to graduating, I became involved with experiential trainings to help people more deeply understand themselves and their behaviors. I continued these leadership trainings over the next seventeen years. These courses planted the seeds that would eventually change my life, and the lives of many others.

It was in these trainings that I became more involved with mindset work and understanding the story creation that happens in our mind. I learned how we identify with the mind's talking and constant programming and evaluating, to the degree that we believe that the stories we tell ourselves are true. And we carry these stories into the world through our behavior, which then creates our reality. I didn't know what it was called yet, but I learned to recognize this inner voice talk as the storyteller. The trainings allowed me to practice coaching others and pull the storyteller to the forefront of their awareness. This process sharpened my skills in recognizing not only the storyteller, but also the inner judgment aspect.

At that point in my personal development, I realized that I didn't need to limit my geographical location by the job I had, because I could live anywhere I wanted. My vision also saw my children having a better life and opportunities than I had, including an education in a better school district. With that awareness and freedom to choose what I wanted, I moved to the South Bay area of Los Angeles.

I was also following the possibility of love. After healing from heartbreak, I was ready for the opportunity to fall in love again and build a family with my kids.

After months of extensive training and coaching, I received my certification in Breakthrough Coaching. I went on to receive my certification in hypnotherapy, and sometime later, I earned a master's degree.

I was breaking boundaries and proving my worth with my love to write. I thought that having my writing published would prove how good I was, and I became a contributing writer in a book called, *Sexy Without Boundaries.*

One of many valuable learnings from my various studies as a coach was about how the body is shaped and designed by our mindset and emotions. It records our experiences and beliefs, and the stories we tell ourselves. It mirrors them, along with our emotional and spiritual states.

I integrated this learning in a way that resulted in me becoming the most healthy and fit I had ever been. At the age of thirty-five, between 2013 and 2014, I tested my discipline muscle and endeavored to accomplish something I always wanted to do by participating in the NPC (National Physique Committee) bodybuilding bikini competitions.

In 2014, as I stepped into a career in human resources. It was there that I began to use the leadership courses and develop myself as an executive coach.

After competing, earning my master's degree, completing all of my leadership training, and beginning a solid career, I believed that I had accomplished everything I needed to do. I was finally embracing all of my life's responsibilities, and my children had grown into young adults, living their own lives. I finally reached that place, the life my parents had always wanted to see me have. Still, there was something calling me to seek further.

In being a bodybuilder, I had learned the power of plants as a more premium food source for maintaining a healthy body. That understanding was the doorway to a deeper exploration of plants as medicine. In 2015, I was introduced to plant medicinal healing for mind expansion. I still viewed Ayahuasca, psilocybin, and all of the others as drugs, but I began to look at them with higher regard for the benefits that I was learning about.

At that time, my aunt passed away from uterine cancer at age forty-four. This was a foreshadowing of a related experience I would have years later. I was navigating that loss, as well as the completion of the healing around a relationship breakup. I wanted to find a level of healing and emotional release that my training, education, and therapy had not provided. I needed to go further out than the boxes my logical mind had kept me in.

So, in February of 2016, I went with a group of friends out of state to experience the beneficial medicine of Ayahuasca. This was the beginning of a healing journey that would eventually form another connection with my aunt's cancer experience years later.

My first medicine journey was the most challenging experience of my life, in terms of facing reality, even more so than my near death from cancer and overdose. Those experiences had offered a potential relief of sorts, because, if the reality that my mom and dad had spoken of was true– *that I was never going to be anyone who mattered, that I was someone who always made mistakes and was never good enough for something or someone good*– then dying could have been much easier than facing that reality.

But, in the Ayahuasca medicine visions I experienced, I was shown things that I could never have imagined. I felt emotions– *anger, shame, fear, loneliness, grief, euphoria, joy, ecstasy, hope*– that I had only felt in the privacy of my own home. I had no control over my own thoughts. My mind played tricks on me, creating scenes that were not there, but felt as real and tangible as life itself. The fear and aloneness and loss of control of my own thoughts was so intense and foreign that I decided never to do it again.

What I did not know then was that the fear was just the feeling of being separated from my mind and my body, which I had never consciously recognized before. It was the state of being only the observer/higher self, the Spirit part of me watching the thoughts, stories, beliefs, fears, and my human body as a vessel my spirit was occupying.

At the nudge of my best friend, I decided that I would continue my work with the master plant. She felt that there was more to explore, and I was not about to let her go into that challenging work on her own. So, I followed her.

After my next few journeys with Ayahuasca, my experience went from being my most challenging to my most profoundly freeing. In my work with plant medicine, I was shown that it was time to release the steering wheel of my life and let go of trying to control anything. It was calling me to be a neutral observer of what I needed to see and what area needed to be healed, whether it was my personal healing, my lineage, community and culture, or even humanity as a whole.

I saw that I didn't have to lead my life from a place of proving myself or being logical. It wasn't about earning another degree, or getting a better job, or getting a promotion, or winning a competition, or publishing my writing. I was being redirected to step out of the human "should, prove, produce" programming. I was being guided to give up control and allow Spirit to take the wheel and show me what I was supposed to do.

When I left the first retreat, I shared my newfound awareness with my friends.

*"Isn't it interesting that we spend our whole lives
traveling to find ourselves,
only to come to something like this and realize,
the furthest journey we take is not physical?
It's the journey from our minds to our hearts."*

Chapter Insight - Going Deeper

In the free-falling roller coaster of my cancer experience, I lived under the influence of my observer/higher self, judgment free for the first time. Also, in describing it, I was allowing that higher self to influence the storyteller, beginning to tell the story of my life in a new, higher way.

I had survived the overdose, given birth to my son, and regained a sense of purpose. I had recovered from heart-break and divorce, and survived cancer.

I was also beginning a new journey of proving that I was good enough, worthy of what I wanted, that I wasn't what my mom had warned me about, and that I could accomplish something great. *"I can do bodybuilding. I can get another certification. I can earn another degree. I can become a leader."* In discovering that I could put my life back together, I saw that I was a good mom, a good student, a good employee. I realized, *"I'm actually good. I'm a good person. I'm good enough."* I was beginning the process of breaking out of the control of my overpowering judgment aspect.

I continued the work with new sacred practices to embody the higher self and recognize the judgment and the storyteller, which used the body to communicate. Being connected to my mindset and how this affects the body, I was able to tap into the connection to begin playing the guitar and sing at the same time.

The reason I was able to become the fittest and healthiest I had ever been when I was thirty-five is because I learned how our body is shaped and designed by our mindset, our inner voice/storyteller, our inner judgment, and our observer/higher self. The judgment and the storyteller use the body to communicate and, in doing so, the body, face, posture, internal cells, and body parts adjust according to the story we tell, the judgment we have on the story, and the emotions we hold.

Have you noticed that some people change drastically in a period of years, while others don't?

Do you know anyone who changed so much that they no longer look vital or happy, while others look more alive and beautiful, despite the passage of time? Appearance is not only influenced by age, exercise, and diet, but also by the mind's stress, emotions, beliefs, judgments, and traumas.

And, in being used to communicate, the body, face, posture, internal cells, and body parts adjust according to the story we tell, the judgment we have on the story, and the emotions we hold.

Yet, I later faced another layer of truth that showed me that thinking I had to prove myself, and that I was good enough, was still me being influenced by my storyteller and judgment. The loss of control over my thoughts during my first Ayahuasca journey was showing me that I was not my story or my judgment. I was the observer/higher self, looking at the mental constructs that controlled me.

I had not been consciously aware of being separated from my thoughts and beliefs. They had always been that part of me I couldn't see, so I believed they were my very being. They had created the story and judgment of every experience I had had since I was a young child, and this Ayahuasca experience did not fit any story that I had ever had, or could ever imagine. So, being consciously separate from my story and judgment mind for the first time, took me out of control. It was as if those aspects of me were not real, and dying, which was terrifying. And, In trying to cling to the story and judgment parts of myself that were being separated, I felt as if I were dying, as if being severed apart from myself.

After more Ayahuasca journeys and learning what the master plant medicine was showing me and teaching me, I realized that all the choices I had made in working with leadership, mindset, and coaching had been very much controlled by my judgment and storyteller voices. I was being shown what it felt like to surrender to the higher self aspect of me, the part connected to Spirit. And, as I understood and allowed myself to see that I was not attached to my inner storyteller, and I was not the judgments, I felt a connection with the deeper part of myself, the higher self of me, and with all that is. And I was no longer afraid

11

Heart Opening - *Abriendo el Corazón*

And then there is love. Having gotten clear on who I was and who I was not, and finely tuning the value of my word by practicing loyalty, integrity, and self-love, I was ready to find a partner to love and to love me. On cue, in walked Kevin. Tall, dark, and handsome, he was definitely someone people noticed when he walked into a room. Unique and outspoken, he was not a shy wallflower, which was attractive to me.

Shortly after meeting him, I left the country to continue my travels. When I returned, he sought me out. As we started spending time together, we recognized our similar interests in body building and self-development leadership practices. He began openly pursuing me, showing me how much he wanted to provide for me, my children, and my family. He was motivated to do his best for all of us, which endeared me to him and won me over.

Kevin was a man who didn't allow limitations to get in the way. When he wanted something, he went after it. He admired that same sense of relentlessness in me. At the same time, he was competitive, complicated, and challenging. He challenged the norm for everyone and was not easy to please. Yet, he felt familiar and fully capable of providing a life for us.

We purchased a house and, in February 2018, decided to get married. It was a lunchtime affair with a wedding cake dessert, and the beginning of a true adventure.

Although I had created a stable career in Human Resources, I had been toying with the idea of leaving.

Participating in sacred circles and medicine journeys was becoming part of my reality, and I wanted to dive fully into working with my spiritual practices. I saw myself holding sacred circles, cacao ceremonies, and facilitating spiritual coaching. My meditation practices prompted visions of love and gratitude for my new husband, my children, our pets, my family, and my friends. I had developed my intuition to the point that my husband had given me the name, "White Witch."

By my forty-fifth birthday, I had stepped further on my path and fully immersed myself in being in service to others. My focus turned to volunteering in and engaging in healing circles and spiritual retreats. I was committed to consciousness and fulfilled by the open-minded community that surrounded me. The strong brotherhood and sisterhood I was part of was a larger family than I had ever imagined possible.

I learned Reiki and became a certified Level 1 and 2 Reiki healer. That was when I awakened to understand why my hands had always reached for people's injuries and were drawn to people's traumas. It became commonplace enough that my kids knew not to come near me if they were injured, so I would not, unknowingly, press on a wound. Not only did my hands gravitate to physical wounds, but my words hit emotional wounds. After learning Reiki, it all made sense

Working with plant medicines was a miraculous healer and heart opener in many ways. I credit my ability to create a different mindset and incorporate mindful practices of deep meditation to the support of micro-dosing psilocybin. This was a medicine indigenous to my country of Mexico and the lineage of my people. When the individuals in the spiritual healing and medicine circles I worked with could see that I had the capacity to hold sacred space with love and Divine order, I was also invited to serve psilocybin. The first time I was called was a very humbling experience. It connected me with being a keeper and protector of medicine for others. It gave me the realization that this was a calling that had opened for me to give people a way to heal, and I needed to listen.

I give full credit of my guitar playing to my work with plant medicines. Playing guitar was a skill I had wanted to learn for years, and I tried several times and took lessons. I learned a little, but still couldn't really play anything. It was during a plant medicine ceremony in October of 2019 when, after taking a small dose of psilocybin, I received a very clear message to pick up the guitar. My heart wanted to play for Spirit.

I looked up the song I wanted to play on YouTube and started playing the chord that I knew. I switched chords, and after a few minutes, I noticed that I was switching chords and positions more quickly. Looking down at my fingers on the guitar strings, I thought, *"Oh my God, I'm playing this song!"* I was playing and singing, and acknowledging the miracle that was happening. *"Oh man, I can play!"* I felt so amazing. I had found the partner to my singing that I had been wanting my whole life. After the experience of knowing I could really play, I began hiring better musicians to teach me and help me improve.

It was here where I was introduced to cacao medicine, the gold and pride of Mexico. Cacao is a rich elixir of minerals and antioxidants that are phenomenally healing for our bodies, blood circulation, and mood. When I learned that psilocybin and cacao are served together with honey, I dove heart forward into the practice. I found that cacao was a delicious way for me to create a healing ritual that was connected to my roots, and when served with psilocybin or on its own, was an introduction to the sacred heart opening medicines. I wanted to share it with everyone.

Between 2016 and 2019, working with both plant medicines and Spirit, I encountered the deepest soul guidance and mentorship I had ever experienced. My intuition became more in tune, and my life purpose was clarified. I saw all the signs, beginning at my birth, of how everything had been planned for my life path. I was shown the trajectory, and in seeing the bigger picture, I knew that I needed to dive deeper.

I needed to be in service to people, so they could also learn and discover their life paths. Before they could do that, though, they would need to heal. And the only way to help them heal was to be in service through other means, like my coaching. So, in March of 2020, I finally decided that a human resources career, in any capacity, was no longer in alignment with what I was seeking and what I was destined for.

Then the pandemic came and put a hold on my plan to leave my corporate career for spiritual healing work. However, the space of the lockdown gave me the time to get more in tune with my guitar, and I was ready to play it in service. On June 4th of 2020, I was invited to play guitar and sing in the sacred practices at a weekend retreat in the high desert breezes of Joshua Tree, California.

On the last morning of the event, we gathered to conclude our sacred circle and prepare to return to our families. As I stepped out from the maloca (an ancestral longhouse used by indigenous people of the Amazon), the hot sun kissed my face and a gust of desert wind caressed my skin.

And in that instant, I felt a sudden urge to head home. The feeling in my stomach immediately filled me with a surge of energy that bubbled up from the center of my core, radiated out to my extremities, and ended right below the crown at my forehead. That feeling of energy had been somewhat dormant since my early childhood, but had been developing again over the years of re-integrating my spiritual practices. I knew there was something coming.

I headed back into the gathering space and walked up to my friend who was playing my guitar. He was strumming "Dust In the Wind," a song Kevin had wanted me to learn, but I hadn't yet. I told him and my other friends that I wanted to leave immediately. They didn't know why I was so intent, and I couldn't quite explain it, but they were my friends. They had come to understand that they ought to listen when I had feelings or premonitions.

My friends and I typically took separate cars, because I enjoyed the quiet time when I drove by myself. I also liked to control my arrival and departure times. However, that particular weekend was different. My friends had insisted that someone else should drive all of us, and I reluctantly acquiesced. Looking back, I am certain that it was a divinely orchestrated plan for my greater good, as it always is.

Less than fifteen minutes after leaving the desert for Los Angeles, my phone lit up with an incoming call, though none of us noticed. We were deep in conversation, and I had been trying to dismiss the initial feeling I had that morning. It returned to the pit of my stomach, which prompted me to look down at my phone. As I picked it up and saw several notifications of calls from my son, it rang again.

When I answered, he asked me a question that felt the same as the question the endocrinologist had asked me, knowing something I didn't.

"Mom, do you know where Kevin's driver's license is?"

"I don't know, son. Is Kevin asking for it?"

"No mom. The police are here, and they need to see Kevin's driver's license."

"Well, Kevin should have it with him if he went out. But, if he doesn't, then it would be upstairs on our dresser. Did something happen to Kevin?"

"Hold on mom. Let me find the driver's license. We don't know. He was out on his bike."

"He wouldn't head out on his motorcycle without his license, son."

"He took his bike."

"Oh, ok. Was he in an accident?"

"Hold on mom. We found it. They're talking with Kelly."

"Son, let me talk to them. What happened?"

"Hold on mom. They are telling Kelly."

"Is he hurt? Did a car hit him? Did he fall again? Is he ok?"

"Mom... He is dead... Kevin is dead."

Chapter Insight - Going Deeper

Furthering my connection to music and sacred practices fortified my connection to Spirit, which had been somewhat silent since my youth. This opportunity to dive deeper with others who were also seeking the Sacred, put me in connection with a supportive community that provided a safe space for growth.

We need community to thrive and although I had sought and found love through a marriage union. I also continued to find love through community and my own spiritual development. In being open to love and having spent time by myself before meeting my husband, I was able to see myself and allow a different kind of love to enter my life.

Kevin's death was a reminder for me that those we care for the most have the potential to hurt us the most, because we will all come to the end of this life. And in dying, we will inevitably break the hearts of those we leave behind.

12

Flickering Light - *Luz Parpadeante*

"NO!" I threw the phone to the floor of the car and curled into a fetal position. *"NO! NO! NO! NO!"* My friend pulled the car over, and my best friend, Ana, got out of the back seat and came to me. She grabbed my phone and spoke with my son. Then, she held me and told my friend who was driving what happened.

All my thoughts and questions swam around in my head. My friends spoke to me, but the only thing that would come out of my mouth was, *"NO."* I heard them speaking to me, and the words I wanted to say were in my head, but I couldn't speak them.

It was so frustrating, knowing what I wanted to ask, and having nothing come out. In the blur of those minutes, I imagined how people with down syndrome or stroke or another disability feel, trying to talk, but unable. While fully cognitive and capable, the body does not always respond the way we believe it should. The only thing my body could feel was, *"NO."*

When we got back to our house, my home with Kevin, my family and friends rushed to my side to try to comfort me. But, I went straight upstairs and curled up on our bed with our dog Oliver, feeling the impossibleness of it all. The wild wind blew like never before in San Pedro, and the house felt as if it were coming apart, like my heart. Everyone was downstairs for me, but I felt alone and exhausted and cried myself to sleep.

I barely dozed off when I heard our bedroom door knob start shaking. I felt Kevin's presence attempting to turn the knob. I said, *"Just come in. You are not in your physical body anymore."* A loud thud hit the sliding glass door across the room, and my eyelids shot all the way open. Oliver stood on all fours staring at the glass. I got out of bed and walked toward the patio to see what had hit the glass, or what had broken it. But, nothing was there. Nothing physical had hit the door that made that noise, but I knew without a doubt that Kevin's spirit had.

As each day passed after the funeral, the people who supported me went back to their lives. My son finished high school and moved out to live with his dad. My daughter finished nursing school and moved out to live on her own. Everyone left, including my oldest brother who had stayed with me to help.

In all honesty, I pushed people out. I felt damaged, defeated, and exhausted. I didn't know what was next, what to do next. I got down on my knees and raised my hands up to God, not in praise, but in surrender, *"I give up. I am done."*

I asked, *"How did I end up here?"* I had turned it around. I had done everything I needed to do, in order to have no regrets over the things I chose to experience. I had given my all to make my marriage work, as difficult as it was, committed to a man who had very complicated habits. I had forgiven him many times. I had tried everything, because I promised myself to that marriage, and I meant, *"til death do us part."* I just had not imagined that death would come so soon.

I asked myself why I chose the life I chose. If I had been told in advance how my life was going to turn out, I don't know if I would have chosen it. I had been dedicated to my career, my husband, my children, my family, my spiritual practices, and a life of service. I had made mistakes. My life was not perfect, but it was perfect for the choices we had made to make each other happy.

With all of my intuition and connection to the spirit realm, and knowing that there is always a bigger picture in creation, I should have seen that I was being guided to begin again. But, at that moment, I did not know why. I could not see. I was in it.

Life grew quieter in a very slow progression, and the stillness heightened my sense of helplessness. I prayed for something that would ease my pain. Help arrived when my neighbor, Dona, from two houses down showed up at my front door in less than thirty seconds. She had lost her husband many years earlier and became my constant support. Her middle of the night texts were reminders to sleep, and her timing was always on point. Every time my phone lit up with her message, I was wide awake. Her early morning hot coffee deliveries were my promptings to make food, something to eat with our coffee. Because of her, I remembered to eat, instead of stay in bed.

Many occurrences took place over the days, weeks, and months after Kevin's death that showed me his need to assure me that he had not gone anywhere. My mind grappled with the reality of his physical body being gone, and at the same time, I was having a direct connection with him and the spirit realm. I wasn't sure how both human suffering and loss could exist simultaneously with the peaceful knowing of spirit. I went back and forth between each of those experiences, along with the judgment of my life and what I was doing wrong. I felt that the door of connection I had always known existed, was wide open to me. But, my new reality became the healing of my broken heart and facing the future alone.

Feeling Dona's presence eased my loneliness and supported the nurturing that I needed to return to the living. Gradually, I picked up my guitar again. Having all the time with myself and God, music was one of the expressions that created connection for me.

I'm sure that people had opinions about the way I lived my life and judged my choices. In fact, I knew of their judgments. One thing I'm certain of, however, is that no one will ever understand someone else's life, because they are not living it. They are not them. I have come to observe that people judge more harshly the things they have never experienced. Or, they judge themselves so harshly that, in order to accept themselves, they sit on the sidelines watching and judging everyone else participating in life.

I have been judgmental, as well, sitting on the sidelines and pretending that I could do better.

I didn't want to pretend anymore. I needed to know how to do better.

Chapter Insight - Going Deeper

Have you ever experienced something so shocking that you lost control of yourself? This is the higher self aspect taking over the body, the thoughts, the story.

Before my son told me that Kevin was dead, the observer/higher self aspect of me did not have full control of my body. It could only communicate with the feeling of the loss, as opposed to communicating and controlling the body for a more meaningful conversation without the pain.

In the moment my son gave me the news about Kevin, and I was hearing that my partner was gone, the love

I felt triggered the high emotion that surfaces in times like those. That was my higher self revealing itself more to me, coming to the forefront, saying, *"I'm here."* The judgment aspect of me was viewing the situation as horrible, and the voice that normally tells the story couldn't say anything except, *"No. No. No."* The body that tells the story could not talk or even hold itself up. They were all out of control. My higher self, observing it all with peace and love was in control, *"This is where I come in. Allow me to take over. Right now, you just need to feel the pain. Feel the loss. Feel the fear. Feel the love and all of those raw emotions. I got you."*

My reaction in that moment, as well as my behavior afterward, is an example of when the observer/higher self has not been prepared. There are different levels of being in the higher self aspect. When we've taken the time to become aware of this part of ourselves, develop and strengthen it, and practice being it, it's easier to allow it to lead us. But when it is not fully developed, or we haven't been aware of it enough to call in, this is what happens.

I had not been fully practicing awareness of, and presence in my observer/higher self. I was aware of it through the experiences I had in my life, but this was the first time that I was aware that my higher self was there. That was the pivotal moment when I saw that my higher self was coming to my rescue. She was letting me know that I didn't need the storyteller or the judgment guiding me in that moment. I just needed to feel it.

When I dropped my phone and curled into a ball, the inner voice/storyteller and the inner judgment no longer had control of my body. Only the observer/higher self was present, in acceptance of the reality. However, my inner judgment did not want that reality, because it viewed it as wrong, bad, horrible, so it influenced the inner voice/storyteller to say, *"NO!"*

When neither the inner voice/storyteller, nor the judgment aspect, have control of the body, the thoughts, and the story are silent, then only the observer/higher self is in control. And, the person has no choice but to accept the reality of the moment.

The process of grieving Kevin's death took me deeper into my personal healing. It also opened a deeper portal into the spirit realm, to the communication that exists between people and spirits, plants, and animals. This was me accessing my observer/higher self aspect.

It was quite amazing for me to witness, having come from a life of being skeptical and trying to dismiss the spiritual as irrational. I had always had a spiritual connection and knew that it was true and real. But, because of all the judgments, comments, and resistance I had received over my life, in terms of my feelings and thoughts not being acceptable, I couldn't be what I was. So, I created a practice of skepticism. It was almost as if the abused had become the abuser. I didn't want to get picked on and judged, so I became the judge.

Kevin's passing broke my final point of resistance to the existence of Spirit, God, invisible energy, and my theories around the stories/narrative and judgments we carry. His passing also showed me that when we pass, we leave all of our judgments and stories/narratives aside, and we are then only what remains– *the observer/higher self and the unconditional love.*

As my story continues, I will also begin to refer to these three aspects as, the NARRATOR, the JUDGE, and the WITNESS.

13

Revelation - *Revelación*

Death of a partner or loved one does something to the person grieving that no one warns them about. The shock and heart presence makes them vulnerable. My inner intuition was off, and my nervous system was out of balance. The reactions my body and mind were experiencing were challenging. The awareness of the higher self I had connected with at age fifteen was no longer accessible to me. I couldn't decipher when something was good or bad, so I couldn't read situations accurately or easily.

Money does something to many of the people surrounding the person grieving. It opens the opportunistic aspect in them. And when vulnerability and opportunism meet, the grieving person becomes prey for predators disguised as helpers. When people started offering to help, I thought my prayers were being answered. However, I wasn't able to discern between real friends who offered from a genuine place and "friends" who offered with the expectation of something in return. It took me some time to realize that. I trusted so freely and openly that, by the time I realized their true intent in taking, rather than giving, I suffered the collateral damage.

However, that was what I needed, to awaken enough to see the truth of them and me. I began to notice that men were looking at me as prey, and my vulnerability as their ticket into my life.

I had been Kevin's human resources consultant. Though it was part-time, I understood the business enough to take it over when he died. With the support of the female project manager and accountant who were willing to help me, I did my best to operate everything and keep the business afloat.

However, some of Kevin's male business partners and engineers were more out for themselves, and they wanted to take over the business contracts. After stealing business information, they started to deal directly with the businesses, which resulted in cutting Kevin's service out. Business colleagues tried to work around me by going directly to the engineers. Men took advantage. Workers stole contracts. In the end, it was not my business to master, and I could not manage it.

With Kevin gone, his business folding, and no money, I had no idea what I was going to do financially. I wondered what I could do that would allow me to live well and focus on my creative side, facilitate my spiritual circles, write a book, and have the experiences I wanted in life. In receiving coaching from my dear friend, Wendy, and support from my sister tribe, I realized that all I needed was the inspiration of a life-changing idea, and I would be set. With that voice in the back of my mind, I went back to my human resources job.

I entrusted a friend and self-proclaimed "doctor" to take care of my pets and gave him access to our home. After returning home one day, I found that he had stolen my husband's guns, along with other personal items. It was clear that I needed to hand our pets over to friends and family, who could give them the constant care and love they needed, but lived close enough for me to check in.

Over those few months, I had inklings of needing to change something, though what and why were unclear in my diminished state of awareness. One night, I laid awake until the dawn turned the sky to daylight, and I realized that what I needed was a reset. I needed to make myself less vulnerable, less enticing. I needed to create a visible armor of some kind, to protect myself from being easy prey. It seemed the only way to weed out my true friends and counsel from those attracted only to my outer beauty, was to make myself less appealing. I needed to shave my head.

I was so certain about it that I would have done it that very morning, had I not wanted everyone to worry that I had finally lost my mind. When I announced my decision to Dona, she was supportive, as well as wise. She advised me that I needed protection. *"If you can get a group of friends to support you in this process, I will help you shave your head."* She was right. It could have been a reactive impulse, but when she suggested her idea, I acted on it. I needed to do it.

The pandemic was still in effect, and people were distancing. So, the next day, a group of sister friends gathered with me on Zoom at Dona's. Sitting in her backyard with her high frequency-tuned sound bowls, she led us in a beautiful fire ceremony ritual. The glowing rays of the California sun warmed our skin, and we breathed in the crisp air of the ocean breeze.

As Dona handed me a pair of iridescent cutting shears that shimmered in the sun, she said, *"When you are ready, make the first cut. Then, offer it to the fire."* I reached my hand up to the top of my head at the center of my crown chakra, twisted a handful of hair and, without hesitation, cut as close to my scalp as I could. We offered my hair to the fire and watched it immediately go up in the flickering light of the flames and disappear into nothingness.

In the years leading up to Kevin's death, I had committed myself to learning and integrating spiritual and healing practices for my community, and I had conceptualized them for myself. But in shaving my head and in receiving the clarity of the need to make a deep change, I knew that I needed to apply the practices to my own personal healing. On that first day of my reset, I began my journey of self-love. It was time for me to be loyal to myself, date myself, travel by myself, be intimate with myself, and nurture a relationship with myself.

Beginning in February 2021, I embarked on a journey of embracing every healing and self-love practice I knew. Eager to learn new ways of examining them, I began integrating them into my being. At an eco-lodge in Costa Rica, I participated in plant medicine gatherings and shamanic rituals with a community of people like me. It was in that beautiful paradise that I was able to fully embrace the guitar in a new way and connect with my gift for playing music. And I experienced an unconditional love and heart healing that could only be described as God's touch. The community and I were all healing, in oneness together.

One of the ritual facilitators was a shaman who had traveled three days from the top of the mountains to come to us. Spanish was his second language, but he knew enough English to communicate. He handed me a cup made out of what looked like a half dried coconut shell and said, *"Tómese esto" ("Take this.")*. The taste was slightly bitter, and I shuddered until the last drop of amber liquid entered my mouth. He asked me to lay on the mustard yellow and brown cushion, atop the beautiful embroidered tapestry covering the ground inside the lodge. Hearing only the sounds of nature and birds outside, I closed my eyes and he placed two golden coins over each of my eye lids. After dipping what felt like a bouquet of fresh leaves, or soft feathers, into the amber liquid, he brushed it on my entire body. I smelled the sweet fragrance and then felt the cool mist of the liquid on my skin.

As the scent expanded into the entire room, my mind pictured Kevin's funeral. I was there, seeing him lying in his coffin with his eyes shut and his hands crossed over his belly. Watching his body's last few hours on earth again, I desperately wished to trade places with him. But, if anyone could handle death, it was Kevin, not I. I had depended on him.

Ours was the first relationship in which I felt trusting enough to relinquish control. I had been exhausted from being the caretaker in my previous relationships, managing budgets, and raising family. I was grateful to finally feel the faith and blessing of having a partner who could handle the weight of it all. He managed everything so proficiently– *our house, his business, our family*. He liked having the control.

I envied his peace, and I knew what that was. I envied his rest and permanent release of worry about the world. I knew, at that moment, that my cries at his departure were not only cries of my sadness that he was gone, but also my sadness that I was still here.

As my thoughts steeped me in emotion, I heard light drumming at my feet. The beats grew louder and more consistent, and the skin on my legs absorbed the vibration. The drumming moved up toward my heart, and when the shaman began to chant a melodic expression, I felt a sharp piercing through my heart. A vision of elders surrounded me and took me to a place where my ancestors were preparing my body for burial. I knew what the experience was. I was seeing my own death, my funeral. I wept, no longer in sorrow for being alive, but in recognition that I had been dying from the moment he left. I had given up and awoken every day with the hope that no one would notice that I was no longer living.

The shaman removed the coins from my eyes and remained silent. When I finally opened them, he told me that I had been holding a spirit around me, and if I didn't let him go, he would be taking me with him. I had felt Kevin around me every day since his death, but I did not know that others could see him. The sacred and powerful shaman confirmed what I had been feeling for eleven months.

Then, he said, *"Let me show you why your children came to be your children."* At that moment, I saw two bright white beings coming down from the sky with big white wings. I knew that they were my children. God was saying to them, *"This woman has gone through a lot of challenges, and we need someone who will bring light to her."* They had chosen to come together, though not at the same time. They had chosen me as their mother, to show me that I was good enough, that I was valuable, that I was worthy, so worthy that I was blessed with the gift of two phenomenal beings to mother. Their appearance was the recognition I needed to know that I had a lot to live for. They still needed me, and they are my primary reason for living.

When I returned to California, I had a new awareness that my new journey had only just begun. Through my ceremonies with Ayahuasca, I had a new awareness of my purpose. My future was to use my spiritual practices to help others.

I had to be closer to the medicine of the people who understood healing, closer to a stronger spiritual community. I could no longer live in the home Kevin and I had lived in. I needed a fresh start somewhere else, yet close enough to visit my parents and my friends. It was time to move. And San Diego was calling me.

I took stock of everything I owned and decided that it was time to sell it all, or almost all of it. I donated many items, including valuables, to charities to raise funds to help women and children. Everything remaining went into storage. In June of 2021, I moved from Los Angeles to San Diego. Eight months later, I quit my job and left my Human Resources career. Finally liberated from the corporate life, I was ready to freefall into my new life as a spiritual intuitive, breakthrough integration coach, and healing practitioner.

In March of 2022, I had an experience that sent a ripple effect of change, for my future, and the future of others.

In the midst of a deep meditation retreat, I suddenly felt a heightened awareness of the people around me and what they were thinking and doing. The meditation retreats were done in silence, with the facilitator being the only person speaking, chanting, and guiding. Despite this, I could hear people chatting, or wanting to chant and share. A conversation started in my head with a voice judging them. The voice was clear, and it was constant. I couldn't stop it. I didn't understand what was happening, but it intensified to the point of criticizing and judging everybody and everything around me all the time, including me.

With frustration mounting and no idea when it would lessen, I told the voice, *"Just shut up. Shut up!"*

Still, it would not stop. While the energy from the inner dialogue was extremely judgmental and critical, it was protective at the same time, like it owned me and got to choose what it thought was good for me and the way I should feel and think.

I stepped out of the ceremony room and asked a retreat helper for assistance. When I told her what I was experiencing, *"I don't know why this is happening in my head right now. I don't want to think this,"* she asked me to share the specifics of what I was noticing and feeling. As I did, the voice suddenly expanded into a general viewpoint of what I had experienced over my whole life. *"People are selfish. They take up space in my head. Even if I'm not asking questions, they're just talking, trying to insert their thoughts and opinions and comments into my head. No one's giving them permission. Who gives people permission to just give me all this information that I wasn't asking for? What gives anyone the right to violate my privacy, my head space?"*

She listened thoughtfully, considering what I was saying, and replied *"That's interesting. I never thought about that."* I said, *"Yeah, sometimes people just come up and say, 'Oh you look nice,' but I didn't ask them. What gives them the right to even invade my space? I don't want to know what they think of me. I wasn't asking for their opinion."*

Feeling overwhelmed with the possibility that the voice I had just begun to hear was now out of the sealed container and never going to go away, I said, *"I don't know how to make her stop. She is just a judgmental b**** that will not stop talking, and I don't want to hear her anymore. What sucks is that no matter where I go, she's going to be there. She's just going to keep talking, and I don't know how to make her stop."*

The retreat helper couldn't provide the relief I needed, so I went to talk with the retreat facilitator. He asked, *"Well, what happens if you just stop talking?"* I said, *"She's still talking inside my head."* He said, *"And you observe her?"* I said, *"This is me observing her. I'm witnessing this whole thing inside my mind."* He said, *"Okay,"* and he put his hands on my head. I closed my eyes while he did a hands-on reiki and guided my breathing. Then, he said, *"Be with her, and love her."* I started tapping my chest, my forehead, and my third eye, and telling myself, *"Come back. Come back."* The tapping, breathing, and reiki connected with my presence and the voice. And, as I loved her, it all created an energetic shift and quickly brought me back, back to me.

The ceremony had ended, and everyone had left for their private rooms to go to bed. However, I liked being in the ceremony space and walked back to my meditation sleeping mat and laid down. I closed my eyes and fell into a trance-like state.

Immediately, I was shown a very specific layout of the NARRATOR and what that meant, the JUDGE and what that was, and the WITNESS and what the witness was. I was shown where we came from and that we each came here as a witness to experience and evolve this world. We were given these bodies to enable us to live the experience of being human and fulfill our assignments on this earth. God gave us permission to come be the WITNESS to guide our human selves and the vessel or vehicle (body) to do it. We know who we are and where we come from when we arrive (birthed).

However, shortly after arriving, we start being programmed (taught) by the judgment (rules, labels, emotions) and the narration (stories, beliefs, and illusions) modeled and given to us by our caregivers, parents, siblings, and extended family. Then, we start being programmed (taught) by television, books, friends, peers, judgments, laws, schools, and community and world influences. Eventually, we forget all the truth we knew, and we believe all the false reality we are programmed with. In this false illusion, so intensely programmed by the JUDGE and the NARRATOR aspects of human society, we forget that we are the WITNESS and think that we are the JUDGE and the NARRATOR.

We forget the truth, until the day or moment something happens to shake us up. It's typically an experience when we feel true unconditional love, or something breaks our heart open, and we are in that raw, wide-open space where the mind and all judgment and narrative quiets to the miracle of the true presence of all that is. And when we have this epiphany, or jolt, shock, or heart-opening moment that reminds us of the truth, we say, *"Whoa! What happened?"* When this happens, we are in the WITNESS state.

I was shown by Divine guidance that I was being assigned to teach this knowledge to everybody, to make them remember that they're supposed to be living from their WITNESS state. And when they live in that state, they will become conscious of when the JUDGE and the NARRATOR have taken over their life. This awareness will set them free from the imprisonment that the lifelong programming has held them in. When they live from their WITNESS, they can actually control their JUDGE and their NARRATOR from a state of love and conscious remembering. This state of intimate heart remembering will enable them to live the full experience of themselves, in full expression of their human and Spirit perspectives, and carry out their life purpose assignment.

I was so excited to learn all of this and that it was my assignment, that I was afraid to wake up and forget it. Suddenly, I was shown a tiny little chip, the size of a phone sim chip, that looked like a pure white porcelain tile, but much stronger than porcelain, stronger than diamond. She said, *"I'm going to insert this in your brain, because you need to bring it to life."*

Suddenly, I remembered all the people who had talked about being taken by aliens and the movies I had seen with people trying to cut into themselves to find the thing that had been embedded. I said, *"Well, what if I forget? Or, what if it breaks? Or, what if it damages my brain?"* She said, *"Don't worry about it. It's so tiny, and I'm going to bury it so deep in your brain that you're not even going to be able to detect it. You cannot get rid of it. It is your assignment."*

The chip was inserted into my brain, and the information downloaded into me. I tried to see it, but it was so tiny that there was no way for me to access it, or break it, or even see it. When she was done, she said, *"I told you I was going to give you a life-changing idea."*

All of the sudden, I felt a force of energy come back into my body, and my eyes sprang wide open. I quickly turned my head and looked around, wondering where I was and what just happened. The whole time I was not sleeping, I was not sleeping. I was being given the assignment. And, I had to share it.

I walked to my friend's room on the other side of the space and told her what happened. She said, *"I can totally see it."* When I went to my other friend and told her, she said, *"Oh my gosh. That makes so much sense!"* I said, *"It does. I need to teach it."* My other friend said, *"You need to go write it down right now."* I said, *"You're right!"* I grabbed my journal from my meditation mat and walked to the candle in the middle of the room. Laying down on the carpet under the light of the candle, I feverishly wrote every detail and nuance of my experience. I didn't want to forget any of it.

For all the years up to that point, I'd been doing all of the work. I'd been opening my heart, healing, serving others, and living my purpose. I received a very clear knowing that it was God saying, *"Now I can trust you to bring this message forth. I'm going to give you all of this information, and I'm going to insert it into you, because I don't want you to let it go. It is that important. It needs to come to life."*

This is universal wisdom that needs to be brought to the consciousness of humanity. The "assignment" may take on different titles or forms or understandings, but it is for all of us to know and share with others. It was my "assignment," but if I didn't do it, someone else would.

Chapter Insight - Going Deeper

I looked back at all the inner judgments I was hearing at the meditation retreat, especially *"I don't know how to make her stop. She is just a judgmental b**** that will not stop talking, and I don't want to hear her anymore... no matter where I go, she's going to be there..."* And, I see that it was the accumulation of the judgment I had been pro-grammed with all of my life, all the females in my family and my mom and her shouldn'ts and taboos. It was all the judgments and story narratives that I was influenced by all of my life.

And the protective nature I felt around the voice was the inner voice in each of us that thinks it's part of us and, therefore, responsible for protecting us, keeping us alive, like a mother.

The voice in my head narrating all the stories (actions) about the people was the NARRATOR. The critical voice judging all the people was the JUDGE. The JUDGE was allowing the NARRATOR a voice to say all those things. The JUDGE and The NARRATOR were aspects developed in my mind by human influences and programming, but they were not part of me.

They were not The WITNESS. I was and am the WITNESS, finally coming out, claiming its voice, its ownership, and its loving power of my body and mind, as it originally had when I was born.

In the safe and loving space of the meditation retreat, my WITNESS had had enough of the NARRATOR and the JUDGE and was ready to re-emerge. Feeling their existence and control threatened, my JUDGE and NARRATOR fiercely defended themselves by getting louder and louder, to drown the rising of the WITNESS. It was ready to assert its presence and center me in my breath, my body, and my heart. And when I was centered and aware of being in my WITNESS state, I was in control and able to just love and calm the voice in my head, the JUDGE and the NARRATOR.

Tapping and breathing is the process to reconnect with ourselves so that we can come out of our head and back into the body, to be in control and aware that we are the WITNESS. I realized that when we can connect to our physical bodies with our breath, or reiki, or tapping, we can disconnect from the out of control mind, the JUDGE and the NARRATOR.

We can recognize that we are not what lives in our head, that those voices– *the JUDGE and the NARRATOR*– are not who we really are. We don't have to become the JUDGE, and we don't have to be the NARRATOR. We can choose to just observe them and not attach. We can be the WITNESS, the consciousness of truth that lives from the heart. And when we are aware of this, we can also stop violating other people's privacy with our thoughts and words.

When we understand this, we can begin to notice how we are always giving permission for other people's opinions and thoughts to invade us and our sense of peaceful privacy. Every time we turn on the tv, radio, or videos, or when we read articles, books, or social media, we are giving other people and programs the right to invade our space, our body temple. Each time we listen to someone talking who we don't want to connect with, we are giving them permission to change our peaceful center and silence our WITNESS.

I became so aware of how we violate people's privacy through the pollution of sounds, conversations, media, and advertisements. When people start talking to us without permission, they are invading our mental space without permission.

I also knew that expressing the WITNESS in the body through ecstatic dance or sacred embodiment is extremely important. The WITNESS needs to express its innate creative state of flow, through singing, dancing, art, beauty, writing, or being connected to nature.

My overwhelm at the meditation retreat was the straw that broke the camel's back, that brought the revelation, that brought the assignment, that shifted everything. The programming that had held me in the darkness was dissolving, and I was beginning to see the light all around me.

None of my experiences were in vain. Quite the contrary, they were the steps that led me to learning what I needed to know, so that I could be fully equipped and centered in my WITNESS to fulfill my purpose and assignment.

14

Freedom At Last - *Libre Al Fin*

Two months after the meditation retreat, at the end of May of 2022, I took another leap into liberating myself. I went on a ten-day silent retreat in the Amazonian jungles of Peru with others who were seeking deeper wisdom and spiritual insight through the intense medicine healing of Ayahuasca.

The protocol and activities of the Ayahuasca medicine retreat in the jungle is referred to as a "Dieta." Preparation starts months prior, with protocols for the participants to clean the mind and body of meats, junk foods, dairy foods, sugars, caffeine, alcohol, and medications. Three to five days prior to the dieta, participants must stop all sexual intimacy and abstain from sex for the duration of the event and fifteen days after it ends. Abstaining from intimacy was not an issue for me, since I had been practicing celibacy for quite some time.

We were separated into individual "tambos" (open-air cottages), placed a good distance from each other throughout the property. No conversation was permitted, and we are not allowed to touch anyone. This was all about connecting with the self, without the influence of potential energy transmission from others.

Being a city girl, I was unfamiliar with the nature of the jungle and fearful of the wildlife, especially the snakes and spiders native to the area and roaming free in the jungle. I was also afraid to be alone in a dark place. There was no electricity, no internet, no running water, no telephones, no toilets, and no showers or tubs. The nights were intensely dark, and the sounds were intimidating, some more difficult to brave than others. The headlamps, solar lights, and candles I was given to light my cottage were never enough to feel safe. Wild life was around every corner. Alone in the jungle, fear took on a whole other meaning.

We were brought food twice each day, along with a special tea. No other food or snacks were permitted, including any oils, salt, seasonings, processed foods, or beverages other than natural water. As part of the inner body and mind cleaning, we were not to use any deodorant or scented lotions. Without the chemical influences to desensitize our senses, our noses became more sensitive to the smells of everything around us. Everyone lost a lot of weight during the dieta. Our inner bodies became very clean.

Each morning, we were given a handful of Amazonian guayusa leaves to bathe ourselves in the river. We crushed them in our hands and let the pieces fall into the water, creating a fresh, green minty aroma. During the sunlight hours, we were free to explore the land, and I became familiar with the fish in the river and the special variety of birds. I saw the most beautiful, interesting, and large blue butterflies I had ever seen, as well as majestic plants and trees that wrapped my cottage in a protective cocoon. In the evenings, we gathered at the Maloca (ancestral long house) for the Ayahuasca ceremonies. We had the option of remaining in the Maloca overnight, but most of us returned to our own individual tambos afterward.

In my medicine healing, the sacred plant showed me my assignment again, a duty bestowed on me to fulfill my promises, and the confirmation that there was still much more for me to bring to life and teach. I came to fully understand that the promises I make to others and to myself carry a huge responsibility, and that I must honor and fulfill them.

It was in the space of that retreat environment and experience that I was able to embrace solitude and come face to face with the fear that lived in me. I connected with all of the unique plants, frogs, birds, and butterflies, and I eventually considered the spiders my friends. Well, they weren't actually friends, but by the end of the retreat, they didn't seem as frightening. The snakes were still pretty scary, though. I'm grateful that I didn't run into any.

At the end of the ten days of silence, there was a day of closing. Afterward, we all went back to the small town to re-integrate a little before heading back to Lima for our flight back to the states.

Going into the jungle was my final embrace of freedom from corporate culture. When I came back to the United States, I had a fresh outlook and new insight about what I was meant to do. I was meant to bring wisdom, guidance, hope, and light to those seeking to see their wholeness, just as I had needed in my journey to healing.

I was filled with clarity and courage to be open and share the practices I had been incorporating in the previous years of leading circles. Finally confident in my purpose, I was ready to dive fully into the sacred spaces of our gatherings and use my entire skill set, which had expanded considerably, as well as my increasing knowledge, and my deepening love. The intuitive integration coaching sessions, healing practice songs, and reiki energy sessions were all going to be integrated into my private practice. Most importantly, I had become the conscious leader I had been working on becoming for fifteen years, and I was ready to apply myself.

Within that two year period of personal healing were so many experiences and shifts. I began a disciplined practice of meditating, with intentions set every forty days. I held personal cacao ceremonies, sometimes with plant medicine microdosing, to help my mind expand and create new neural pathways. I conducted group cacao ceremonies for women with guided meditation, energy healing, and music. I engaged in intuitive coaching with angel cards, plant cards, and the tarot. I received private one-to-one sacred ceremony sessions. And, I continued to work with plant medicines with shamans and guides.

Releasing and purging excess items minimized my ownership of material possessions and cleared my field. Reading one or two books a month opened my mind to various authors and teachings. Learning and creating new music and chants allowed my soul to express itself. Even if I never shared or wrote the songs, I knew that the simple act of creating and practicing new music was enhancing my mind's plasticity.

With the opening that the 2020 pandemic had created for conducting services virtually, I stepped in to having an online presence for a majority of my coaching practice. Embracing the new freedom of life to go anywhere I wanted, I traveled to many new destinations.

One of the first was Mexico. In receiving the message in my medicine healing that I had a duty to fulfill my promises, one of them appeared front and center in my mind. It had been over thirty six years since my mom had promised to make an offering to the Virgin Mary for saving me at birth, and my life had been saved three more times. I didn't want her and my dad to be too old to travel to fulfill that promise. So, I paid for most of the arrangements, planned the flights and accommodations, and contracted a helper to help my dad get around. The three of us went to Mexico City and completed my mother's "manda" (offering).

I flew to several places in the United States and around the world, some of them more than once, including Costa Rica, Peru, and Jamaica. I traveled to Mexico City, Cabo Mexico, three Hawaiian Islands, Colombia, the Grand Canyon Arizona, New York, Florida, Washington State, New Orleans, Baltimore, Chicago, Connecticut, and Pennsylvania. And my traveling is not finished. Accessing as many places in the world as possible is a practice I'm committed to for my continued healing and purpose.

The gift I received in my journey of exploration, expansion, and deep connection was the gift of wholeness. Healing, reconnecting, and loving the parts and pieces of myself that had seemed to be in shadow, separation, and judgment allowed me to be all of me. And from that alchemized state, I was able to see how my journey had taken me from the darkest of spaces back to the light of my true self. But, I had to follow the light that others shared with me until I could reconnect with and be in my own light. In that place of wholeness, I had created a new foundation on which to be in service for others.

It is a lifelong journey, and I am grateful to be on it. To those who have survived life's intense challenges, people often say. *"Everything gets easier with time."* I don't believe that's true. I believe that we learn to be stronger, in order to live with loss and trauma, and we do that by wholeheartedly embracing our path to healing and passing on the knowledge.

Chapter Insight - Going Deeper

Being in the jungle and fearing the raw nature surrounding me served as a mirror to reflect my shadow, the dark pockets and fear that I had. It was a magnifying glass revealing the jungle we face in our everyday lives. This journey was my WITNESS directing me to see the fear and where it came from and embrace it.

When we look at the process of healing, we sometimes evaluate, JUDGE, it as a struggle, a heavy and difficult burden. We can miss the higher viewpoint, WITNESS, that knows that looking at our darkness, or shadow, of past failures, traumas, and fears is what evolves us and strengthens our sovereignty. Revealing our shadow is vital to revealing our light.

When we shy away from the things that scare us, we block our opportunities for growth and discovery of our life purpose and assignments that we came to complete. Opening to the darkness and danger of the jungle, along with my assignment of responsibility for my integrity, allowed the light to be revealed. When I surrendered to the beauty and healing wisdom of the plants, I was able to expand out of the fear and claim my assignment and life purpose.

Looking back at those moments of life-altering trauma, bone-chilling fear, and heart-breaking loss, can you see that was you, coming face to face with your darkness. And, can you look now and notice that there was a glimpse of Light seeping through the cracks of the broken pieces? That was your higher self, ready and waiting to begin the healing and the revealing of your life purpose.

"The two most important days in your life
are the day you are born
and the day you find out why."
-Mark Twain

15

Illumination - *Iluminación*

The sliding glass door of my bedroom in my new home revealed a gorgeous view of the San Diego canyon. I loved falling asleep to the city lights far below and waking to the sunlight shimmering through the shades. One of my favorite things to do when I awoke was stand outside to view the breathtaking nature that surrounded my home and pray for my children, my family, and my friends. Then, looking down at the traffic and buildings, I liked to reach my hands out and open them to the city and have a conversation with the energy of the people in it. I liked to pray for them and ask them, *"Do you know that I am trying to make this world a better place?"* And, then I always affirmed, *"You want to support me. I am doing my best to leave this world better than I found it."* And with that, I began my day with trust that my message was being received.

I practiced my daily meditation sitting at the center of my living room, which had the same view of the canyon. One morning in October of 2022, after leading a weekend circle, the city was muted by a veil of clouds that gracefully skimmed the ground just below the trees. The veil allowed my meditation to deepen, and a vision appeared of a woman made of shiny white porcelain meditating in lotus pose. Her eyes were closed, so I stared at her body and noticed that it was laced with tiny beautiful shimmering strands of gold.

As I looked closer, I noticed that the shimmering was not strands, but the light inside her seeping through tiny cracks all over her body. It seemed that she had been put back together by a crafty artist. But her light was so bright that it could not be contained inside of her, nor dimmed by her reconnected pieces. I stared at her stillness, wondering how she had been put back together after what appeared to have been a massive destruction obliterating her from the inside out. I wanted to know how nothing was holding her pieces in place.

As I studied her, her eyes opened, startling me. She did not pay attention to my stares and reached her delicate right hand down and across her body, and with beautifully crafted fingers, picked up a large piece of porcelain that had fallen from her abdomen. I watched her place the last piece back perfectly on herself to cover the hole that illuminated her inner glow. Then, she repositioned her hand on her knee and returned to her peaceful pose.

It was suddenly clear that she was the one responsible for putting her pieces back together, not a crafty artist. I continued to watch– *with my heart, not my eyes*– and I knew. She didn't need any glue. The true essence of her, the WITNESS, could never fall away. That was what made her indestructible. She may have appeared fragile, but she had the ability to rebuild herself each and every time a piece fell. And she emanated peace, love, and grace while doing so.

What struck me more powerfully than anything was that the cracks from her broken pieces were what allowed her light to shine outward so brightly. As I looked at her, I thought, *"Her light is seen from every point of view. Ella es una lanterna que guia" ("She is a guiding lantern.")*. Like a lantern, no matter what angle the beholder viewed her from, her light was always visible. The cracks from the towers that had tried to destroy her actually magnified her radiance.

It was like the veil of clouds outside my window that day. Some would be depressed, because they covered some of the light, and others would meditate in the quiet of the clouds and wait for the light of illumination. Some people would view the woman as broken and damaged, and others would see her as I was seeing her, a light guide to remind us that nothing and no one can take away our light.

I opened my eyes and placed one hand over my heart and the other on my abdomen. *"This could be me,"* I thought. *"This could be any of us. We can choose to see ourselves as broken and focus on the damaged parts. Or, we can pick up our pieces and put ourselves together with the brighter light of the wisdom we gained."*

With new sight from this vision, I was grateful for the message reminding me what happens when we choose to see our wholeness, our light. I recognized that the cracks from the fallen towers that could have destroyed us, are actually gifts that crack us open and reveal the light inside of us.

Each of our cracks is a mark from an experience that has stretched us, to birth a new awareness. And, each new awareness brings light. When we seal ourselves so tightly, out of fear, anger, shame, or sorrow, we become impenetrable to the light of our own awareness, and we can't see it. When we learn to rebuild ourselves, or allow others to help us put back our pieces, we can see our wholeness. In accepting our cracks, rather than hiding them, and in loving them, not shaming them, we allow them to reveal our indomitable light.

And the light is visible even in those who have not yet rebuilt themselves. It is seen in the beauty that emanates from their voice, the light in their eyes, the warmth in their touch, and the soul of their creations. But my heart resonates with those who continue to commit to the complete rebuild, with those who practice the sacred walk of the reborn, and with those who allow their light to shimmer through every crack.

Chapter Insight - Going Deeper

When we connect with our own insight, we can become aware of the moment when our innate understanding began deconstructing. And when we do this, we connect with our Light and become the WITNESS of our healing.

In rebuilding myself, I was able to have that vision of the illuminated woman and what she represented. It was through the support of my community brothers and my sister-friends of seventeen years, both blood related and spiritually connected, that I had been able to grow in strength.

It was with the presence of my parents showing me how to WITNESS day in and day out, even if they were not there physically all the time. It was in being a WITNESS that I was able to be a part of a community of fellow WITNESSES. It was through being WITNESSED by others that I was able to re-member myself. It was all of this that allowed the perfect timing for me to vision the lady, who showed me how to look at myself. She was my WITNESS reminding me that I had always been whole, that nothing could ever break me.

PART THREE

SPIRITUAL RESOURCES

RECURSOS ESPIRITUALES

Over the last few decades, I've explored many modalities, methods, rituals, and practices in my journey to self-love and healing, and in my work with others. In the final three chapters, I share a recent journey of healing and a few resource recommendations, including my revelation that inspired this book, **The ITMYS™ Method.**

16

Miracle Plants - *Plantas Milagrosas*

As part of rebuilding my life and seeking a path of healing, I opened myself to a new relationship with a partner who shared my focus on healing and spiritual practices. Nurturing this new relationship and allowing it to flourish, I put my relationship with myself in the backseat.

In navigating my new self in romantic partnership again, I became challenged with maintaining a balance between the intimacy that I had cultivated with myself and intimacy with my new partner. It was creating an energetic and emotional instability around my worthiness, not standing up for what I wanted, and putting myself second. Thinking that he wasn't stepping up emotionally had the effect of disconnecting me from him and creating resentment.

He started being more of a caretaker, emotionally reassuring me, and supported my healing.

With a mutual intention to expand our individual healing journeys, as well as seek a deeper connection with one another in partnership, we decided to attend a silent retreat. In October of 2023, we traveled into the jungles of Peru to do the deep work of a medicine journey.

While all of this was happening, I was having a lot of issues and pain in my uterus that came and went. The doctor had given me some fungal medication, but it wasn't working. I tried boric acid, moisturizing inserts, antifungals, probiotics, and everything that I could try.

Nothing was working. This was yet another opportunity to understand the mind-body condition.

When we arrived, I began fasting, per the protocol for the Ayahuasca dieta. Each of us at the retreat was in separate tambos, completely separate from any other person's resonance and vibrational frequency and influence. Because we were separated from other humans, we were purely in our own essence and energy, in connection with the full impact of the jungle's medicine, the plants, the ground, the water, and the animals. I had already known that the jungle is nature's hospital.

Under the revealing influence of Ayahuasca, I noticed that every time I got near my boyfriend, my uterus started to burn. The medicine was highlighting the level of resentment and emotional hurt that I was feeling toward him. It was showing me where I was holding all of the energy and frustration.

As the Shaman was facilitating my healing, I closed my eyes and was instantly shown images of injustices, victimization, and people being conquered, massacred, and abused. All of that rage, my own and that of the collective, was being turned to me, going into me. Feeling the intensity and potency of it all, I knelt on the earth, pounding both fists on my knees, and shouted, *"No! No!"* I felt so helpless and hopeless in being able to do anything for any of those people, including myself.

The next morning, I received another dose of medicine. With eyes closed, I started seeing flickers of light shimmering behind me through the back of my head. I thought it was mother Ayahuasca showing off. Her spirit was red and black, part tribal, part sacred geometry, like a snake kaleidoscope. I said, *"You're so beautiful."* She swirled in and out and around, and when she stopped, the flickers of light within her swirls revealed her mermaid-like shape. Pearly white, like mother of pearl, she shimmered in iridescent green, pink, and lavender, and her skin was covered in scales like a fish. She had big slanted eyes and a tiny nose, a pointed chin face and a long tail with a big diamond at the end. Her head at first looked like a crown, but as I looked closer, I saw that it was her skeleton covered in the mother of pearl scales.

She came out from behind me and stopped right in front of my face, holding her hands up next to her head. They looked amphibious, like the hands of a gecko, and she said, *"I'm Bobinsana. I'm here to help."* I said, *"Please help me."* She said, *"I will, but you are trusting in Western medicine."* I said, *"I know. I'm just in so much pain. Please, please make it stop."* She said, *"Okay, I will help you."*

As she turned around, I could see the back of her head and skeleton all covered in the beautiful mother of pearl scales. She moved down to my belly and stopped right in front of my sacral chakra and said, *"I need your permission."* I said, *"Please, please help me."* She said, *"Okay."* And with that, she dove right into my uterus.

I heard a loud noise in the jungle and opened my eyes. I was back in my room. I didn't know how I got there, but I wanted to see her again. So, I closed my eyes, but she was gone. I felt so much love at the sight of her that I hurried to my journal so I could draw her image.

I went to the Shaman to tell him that another plant spirit showed up. He said, *"Who showed up?"* I said, *"Bobinsana."* He said, *"Are you taking that medicine?"* I said, *"No, I'm taking Shihuahuaco."* He said, *"Wait, she showed up for a reason. What's going on with your uterus?"* I came clean to the Shaman and told him what was going on and that I had felt a lot of burning in my uterus during his healing over me the night before. I told him that I noticed that the emotions came up when I came near my boyfriend and that I thought there was something more serious going on there, because I was in a lot of pain.

The Shaman spoke with the Vegetalistas, the Medicine Men who prepared the brews, and they switched my medicine to Bobinsana. Bobinsana is a healing plant that brings moisture, suppleness, and elasticity back to our bodies. They also gave me a vaginal wash called Chuchuhuasi made of seven different plants to insert every two hours. Bobinsana and Chuchuhuasi are not psychoactive plants or psychedelics. As soon as I took the new medicines, a powerful peace came over me, and I felt so much better.

On the day off from ceremonies, I walked down to the river to bathe and wash my clothes. After washing my underwear, I set them to dry on a large rock next to the river, and two beautiful yellow butterflies immediately landed on the crotch of my underwear. They were clean, so there was no scent on them that would attract any insects. Both butterflies stayed right there. It felt like a sign from Spirit saying, *"You're going to be okay."* I was filled with such gratitude, relief, and amazement that I started crying.

As I did, I saw a huge brown, white, and black bird with an orange beak on my left across the small river. Its long orange feet walked very gently, then it stopped and sat watching me while I cried. The butterflies on my right and the bird on my left sat for forty-five minutes without moving as I cried and bathed in the river. They did not go anywhere. They just stayed there holding space for me. It was as if they said, *"She needs to cry, and she needs to not be alone. And we're doing that for her."*

Finally able to face the current of the river, I lay in it and said, *"I am ready to receive everything that is meant for me: the love I deserve; the respect I have earned; the trust I uphold; the integrity I honor; and the financial abundance I source. Because I am a funnel for all good. I receive it."* As I lay on a rock and let all the river water cover me and my hair, the rain hit my face, my belly, and my chest, and my legs were not fully submerged. *"I am so very grateful."* Later that day, I wrote in my journal. *"It's raining. Wonderfully amazing thunderstorm. I just came back from bathing in the river with the rain falling on me. I used to dream of getting caught in the rain with my beloved. Now I realize, my beloved is me."*

For a month after we returned to the U.S., I continued inserting the Chuchuhuasi medicine, and then I visited the doctor. They took all kinds of STD tests, a pap smear, and a culture, and said, *"There's nothing here. Everything is clear. You're good to go."*

A "Miracle" is defined by humans as something unexplainable by natural or scientific laws. In truth, miracles are the reality of Spirit in action. When we live in the consciousness of our higher self, the WITNESS, we have access to the energy that continually creates them.

In the journey to the jungles of our Ayahuasca retreat, we had driven four hours from Pucallpa into the jungle. There were no buildings out there, no lodging, only land. The man who owns the property had been imprisoned for two years for transporting Ayahuasca. He was released last year and sat with us in October, along with other Shipibo tribe elders. I had the honor of meeting him and translating what he was saying to the tribe. One of the things he said in recalling his release was especially powerful.

"The judge said, 'You know sir, the only thing that would save you right now would be a miracle.' I said, 'Well Your Honor, the thing about us spiritual people is not that we be-lieve in miracles. The thing about us spiritual people is that we count on them."

- Don Jose

Chapter Insight - Looking Deeper

The vision of the illuminated porcelain lady I had one year prior to this trip to the jungle was a sign from my WITNESS. I remember thinking, *"This could be me… We can choose to see ourselves as broken and focus on the damaged parts. Or, we can pick up our pieces and put ourselves together with the brighter light of the wisdom we gained."* Picking up the last piece of her porcelain ab-domen that had broken off was a foreshadowing of the "broken" piece of my body, my uterus. Like her, I put my last broken piece back on.

The uterus is the sacral chakra energy center, the place we hold emotions and the womb where we create from passion. It is the element of water, where we birth life from our desire for expansion.

This area is also where we hold trauma. Over my life, I experienced much suppression, as a result of my over controlling JUDGE that had been programmed and strengthened by others, and myself. A great part of that suppression was from the rape I had experienced when I was sixteen. After all those years, my repressed pain and anger (inflamed, red, rage) was no longer able to be kept quiet. It was calling my attention.

The plant medicine, the WITNESS, at the retreat was highlighting those wounds that needed to be healed, and it was actively working on doing that. But, even before I arrived at the retreat, my body was showing me, with the physical pain and emotional discomfort. This was my NARRATOR, under the influence of my WITNESS. It was giving me the message that I had unexpressed emotions, repressed sensuality, and suppressed creativity that were ready to be expressed (seen and let out).

In those fifteen days before the jungle, eleven days in the jungle, and fifteen days after, I was nurturing my self-love. Allowing the plants and creatures to be in a relationship with me, the Spirit of the plants to heal me, and the river and rain to nourish me. I was healing my last broken piece. Being with myself, my beloved me, was my dream.

Looking back, I am reminded of my aunt's death from uterine cancer in 2015. She had endured sexual traumas as a young woman and had a child who was the product of a gang rape. My aunt later got married and had two more children with her husband. She tried to live a normal life; however, she suffered from her husband's infidelity. Eventually, her long held suppression, her inner JUDGE, and her lack of forgiveness led to the dis-ease of uterine cancer. Eventually, she died from the unhealed dis-ease, still under the influence of the JUDGE and NARRATOR, the betrayal, anger, and unexpressed pain. The last words she spoke were to her husband, telling him that he was free to sleep with whomever he wanted.

When we have spent our lives disconnected from our WITNESS, we are not in our innate Spirit of ease, and our bodies begin expressing this dis-ease through ailments. Remaining in this state of dis-ease is what eventually kills the body, the human vessel we are living our human experience in. Then, the Spirit leaves the body (body death). This is the endpoint of resentment and emotion held within and unexpressed. Most times, we are not even aware that we are doing it, or that we are creating our own death sentence.

But, if we catch ourselves, if we choose to open our hearts and reconnect with our WITNESS, we can reconnect with ease and flow and return to health. The way to heal and unlock the flow (the dam) is to allow ourselves to express (surface, let out) our trapped emotions (water, air, or fire energy). This is the process of allowing the NARRATOR to do what it needs to do and say what it needs to say, free of the influence of an overactive JUDGE. We can do this through deep breathwork, crying, laughing, dancing, singing, or even playing an instrument. It is vital for us to be connected with our WITNESS, so that full self-expression and trauma energy are allowed to flow and move through and out of our bodies.

17

The ITMYS™ Method
In To Me You See™

The Code of Creating True Intimacy in All Relationships: (Sisterhood, Brotherhood, Parenthood, Friendship, Business, Marriage, and Self)

Navigating all of life's experiences:

(Overcoming Grief, Accomplishing Goals, Healing Traumas, Reconnecting with Life Purpose)

And leading business:

(Organizations, Teams, Developing and Influencing Self-Discipline)

Through the years and experiences of my life and healing journey, I developed the understanding of the three aspects of the human and how to identify each of them. In late 2022, I trademarked **The ITMYS™ Method.**

The ITMYS™ Method supports my effectiveness as a coach in helping others develop a deeper self-awareness and understanding, embrace the consciousness of leading themselves, and create deeper intimacy with themselves and those they seek to have relationships with.

The basic structure begins with the recognition of the presence of the following three states embodied in each human and his/her experience: The NARRATOR; The

JUDGE; The WITNESS. These can be considered the "points of views" that exist within our individual psyches.

Being conscious of these components or points of views can impact the way we perceive ourselves, others, and life. Understanding the roles and purposes of the NARRATOR, The JUDGE, and The WITNESS can be a gateway to accessing the higher consciousness available to all human beings.

The NARRATOR is the "inner voice" of the human, the "storyteller" that details everything that we see, think, feel, and experience. The NARRATOR can be noticed when we are simply going about our day. It is the voice that speaks, narrates, or describes everything we do. The NARRATOR is the point of view that is continually trying to create an understanding of our experiences.

The NARRATOR expresses itself by making the body move, speak, write, or sign (communicate). In more detail, The NARRATOR has the ability to describe what the body is doing, feeling, thinking, or experiencing, through words, thoughts, or motion, such as body language, expressive movements, or sign language.

The NARRATOR can be seen as words on a screen in our mind, heard as an inner voice, or expressed through writing or body motion. This component of the human normally expresses itself through the language dialects humans identify with worldwide. We recognize it through the language we used most in our upbringing.

The limitation of The NARRATOR is that it can only pull from what the individual's conscious mind knows, such as past experiences, past learnings, and past constructs. It will give us a sense of the world that is in line with what we know up to that point. It can only narrate from that context. It cannot go out of the box or into the realm of possibilities or unknown.

The NARRATOR can be influenced by the JUDGE and can even utilize it to benefit its expression.

The JUDGE is the "evaluator" of the human and the aspect we most identify with. It is the point of view that JUDGEs situations, applies discernment, and makes decisions. We think this is what defines our human experience. We choose education, careers, partners, and experiences from The JUDGE component, and we identify it as our source for determining right and wrong, good and bad, weird and normal, strong and weak, smart and dumb, acceptable and unacceptable. It is highly influenced by our upbringing, cultural history, gender identification, religious beliefs, and socio-economic status.

The JUDGE has a high influence on the NARRATOR. The JUDGE uses the NARRATOR as an inner voice to tell us, *"You should do this,"* or *"You should not have done that."* The NARRATOR can be neutral and pull what it needs from its database, but The JUDGE can be critical and will formulate meaning to control the conscious mind by what it deems right, good, smart, strong, acceptable.

The JUDGE seeks to protect us in all aspects of survival, both emotional and physical. Those who live by the voice of The NARRATOR can be so strongly defined by The JUDGE, that their human experience is run from a belief that they need to be physically and emotionally protected from harm.

The JUDGE can strongly influence The NARRATOR to the extent that it can overpower The WITNESS, sometimes to the extent that The WITNESS appears non-existent.

The WITNESS is the "neutral observer/higher self," of the Human, defined as higher knowing, consciousness, and intuition. The WITNESS is the omniscient point of view, all-seeing and all-knowing. It knows that it is neither The NARRATOR nor The JUDGE.

It seeks to connect through love, beauty, meaning, connection, impact, purpose, inspiration, self-expression, compassion, and magic. We can be aware of The WITNESS during heightened states of physical or emotional pain, including child birth, death of a loved one, near death experiences, shock, heartbreak, great tragedy, or accidents. We can also notice The WITNESS in times of excitement and peak experiences, such as during deep breath work, meditation, out of body experiences, passionately working toward a goal, and competitions. And we can experience The WITNESS during inspirational sessions and emotional release expressions, like music, poetry, art, play, creative work, dance, unconditional love, forgiveness, and sexual orgasm with a loving partner.

These states and times create a chemical release in the brain that naturally occurs when the pineal gland is activated. The WITNESS, the "observer/Higher Self," then has the opening to take over The JUDGE (the Human "Mind"), and The NARRATOR (the Human "Body").

Guide to The WITNESS Descriptions: The use of the word "aware" is interchangeable with any of the following words: "awakened;" "defined;" "fully actualized;" "realized;" or "developed." The word "undeveloped" is interchangeable with "diminished;" "unawakened;" "unactualized;" "unaware;" or "undefined."

When we are aware of The WITNESS and understand how it communicates with The NARRATOR and The JUDGE, The WITNESS can consciously influence The NARRATOR and The JUDGE for our full self-expression.

When The WITNESS is not fully actualized or even highly defined, or when it has been diminished by The JUDGE or overpowered by the loudness of The NARRATOR, we lose awareness of its existence, and can then only see glimpses of it during strong experiences that are beyond expression or judgment. In other words, The WITNESS in us then becomes identifiable only during emotions and experiences that are so overpowering that they have quieted The NARRATOR and The JUDGE, and The WITNESS is the only presence we are aware of.

Awakening and Living from The WITNESS

If we live from The WITNESS state, we can call into form (physical manifestation) the connection we "feel" with others, beyond language, time, or space. This is when we notice coincidences after "thinking" about someone or something and that event happens or that person appears as we imagined or predicted.

When The WITNESS in us is aware, it can manifest, act through, influence, and control The JUDGE and The NARRATOR. In this state The WITNESS is able to actively seek connection with and communicate with other fully expressed WITNESSes in our human experience.

When The WITNESS is not awakened within us, The JUDGE and The NARRATOR will run, control, act, influence, and create our human experience. This way of existing then denies our deeper connection with others, especially if those others also have an undeveloped, diminished, or undefined WITNESS.

When humans begin seeking deeper meaning and connection, they will relinquish control of The JUDGE and The NARRATOR to The WITNESS. As they do this, they will begin to connect with other WITNESSes and create opportunities for The WITNESSes to experience each other and truly see the essence and full self-expression in each other. This is the ability to bear WITNESS to others' full self-expression and human potential. Allowing ourselves to experience the world through The WITNESS is our gateway to higher consciousness within our human experience.

18

Other Practices and Rituals
Otras Prácticas y Rituales

The practices and methods you engage in on your spiritual journey of awakening are a personal choice you must make for yourself. They call each individual differently. Be open to listen to the messages. Be open to see the signs given, the breadcrumbs on your path. The sign might be hearing someone talk about something they experienced and feeling a strong desire to try it. The message might be reading something that clearly inspires you and feeling it in your body. Often, it's a nudge or intuition that you've felt, or heard, for weeks, months, or years, and its whisper seems louder. If you've heard the message two or three times, that's your inner guidance leading you there.

Pay attention to dreams and what they show you. They reveal patterns, desires, and premonitions. Your body tells you what feels good and right and true for you, by guiding you to stop or start or move or change. It knows. If you've felt compelled to do something or go somewhere, follow the feeling.

We can actually ask for guidance and be given confirmation of our interpretation of what we received. Be open to spiritual contact. That contact can come in many forms. The higher the feeling and excitement, the more you can be certain of the confirmation that the Universe, God, Spirit is listening.

Healing Circles - Attend sacred circles in which you're able to grow spiritually as a vital part of your journey. Growing within a conscious community, where you can have deep conversations of faith and connection, is a gift. You can also connect with a community by joining my mailing list through visiting my website: https://cinthiagambino.com/

Meditation Rituals - Practice connecting with your higher guidance and emotional healing through meditation and visualization. These practices support us in releasing anxious and depressive thoughts and trauma. Look for resources to support you in connecting with yourself and your life purpose in a way that you won't be distracted from your walk, your breathing, and nature. Breathing meditations, walking meditations, movement meditations, gratitude meditations, group meditations, and 40-day goal-setting meditations are all avenues that bring you into connection with your body, the earth, and Spirit. Any of these can become a transformative ritual. Eating, bathing, singing, chanting, painting, writing, cooking, or cleaning, when done with presence and gratitude, can bring you into a constant meditative state. If you're interested in doing a 40-day meditation ritual, I can support you as a coach to integrate the practice: https://cinthiagambino.com/

Manifestation Practices - Build hope, confidence, and manifestations into reality through positive thoughts, vision boards, journaling, envisioning, affirmations, and other practices. When your mind has a roadmap of your place in time, it can more easily lead you there. You can also work with me one-on-one, or join my mailing list, https://cinthiagambino.com/, to join virtual events or access my practices.

Medicine Retreats - Consider participating in sacred cacao, psilocybin, mescaline, or Ayahuasca retreats. They are extremely liberating, revealing, and healing. These holistic plant medicines are the basis of my coaching work. It's important to research, however, so that you find a trusted teacher who holds these practices with respect, honor, safety, and sufficient support staff. For resources and events, you can join a resource mailing list through my website: https://cinthiagambino.com/

Love and Forgiveness - Practice the Hawaiian Ho'oponopono to open your heart and shift your emotions, body, relationship, health, and life back into balance and harmony. Love, forgiveness, and gratitude are the highest emotions for transmuting difficulties in any area of life.

Embodiment - Strengthen the presence of the heart-centered WITNESS, and nurture its expression by practicing activities that bring you into flow. These practices allow the spirit to take over the body and mind and fully express itself, without the influence of the NARRATOR and JUDGE. One of these practices is Ecstatic Dance, dancing as wacky as the spirit wants. Another is EFT, tapping the body without judgment, which reminds the WITNESS that it has full control of the body vessel. Breathwork is another life-changing practice. The foundation of the NARRATOR and the JUDGE acts from survival, not consciousness. In breathwork, breathing becomes intentional, rather than a process of unconscious survival. Taking deep, full breaths becomes the focus of the WITNESS.

Group Coaching - Create connection with your spiritual "tribe" (community) to expand your awareness, strengthen your self-love practices, and refine your intuition. I offer Group Coaching Cohorts several times a year. You may sign up for these classes through my website and Instagram: https://cinthiagambino.com/ https://www.instagram.com/cinthiaveronicamsm.

The ITMYS™ Method - Practice recognizing the three inner aspects of yourself, the JUDGE, NARRATOR, and WITNESS. In this awareness, you can actively choose to live as the WITNESS in your human experience and create a life that is worthy of you, not the other way around. You can work with me through my one-on-one intuitive integration and leadership coaching at https://cinthiagambino.com/

ITMYS™ 12 Week Journal - You may feel called to begin your new journey now and step into the embodiment of In To Me You See. To facilitate this, I'm offering a FREE ITMYS™ 12 WEEK JOURNAL to use as a tool for Creating a Life Worth Living. Email me to request your journal: cinthiaveronicamsm@gmail.com

EPILOGUE
Call to Action

Using spiritual resources, messages, and guidance is not just a one-time occurrence, but an ongoing practice we can continue to embrace. Use this book as a tool to practice as many times as you need to. And don't limit yourself to this book. Look for other resources and teachers to learn how to connect with your wisdom and the guidance that is available to you.

Just as important, don't seek so much that you get stuck in the seeking. Incorporate the practices, take the steps, and take action. The Universe, God, Spirit gives infinite opportunities and possibilities to us, but if we're all talk and don't do anything with them, we're not going to go very far. We can be smart, yet not wise. Knowledge is great, but wisdom is gained only when we apply the knowledge.

Thank you for taking this journey of reading my story and **The ITMYS™ Method** - In To Me You See. I know that your insights along the way also helped You to See In To You. Crossing the bridge to understanding the three aspects of yourself is a triumph. Coming to this awareness is not easy. Maintaining it is even less so.

Whether you are the parent, the employee, the student, the partner, or the dreamer, you are being called to choose to lead your life. Leading means consciously choosing, creating the reality you want to experience, speaking your experience into reality, and stepping deliberately in the direction you want to go

Most humans have been unconsciously doing the opposite their entire lives, randomly being bounced from one situation, place, program, and person to another, by default. We've been conditioned to allow another force, person, belief, or aspect of ourselves, JUDGE or NAR-RATOR, to influence us into a direction, without truly desiring to go there.

Each of us creates the story with our own energy, whether our energy is awake and intentional, or uncon-scious and unintentional, allowing ourselves to follow the influence, even if the influence is negative, or not where we want to go.

When we open ourselves to being the WITNESS and allowing the WITNESS to guide our NARRATOR and JUDGE, we lead from the heart space of non-judgment. We are allowing love to flourish within us and around all that we do. But, to be in the continual emotion of love is not easy to do. People have a challenging time allowing themselves to be love, and be loved, because it feels like walking through the day as a raw nerve, vulnerable to getting hurt.

We have created calluses, armor, walls, and layers of ice around our hearts and emotions, because being frozen, armored, or callused protects us from emotional pain. When we start opening ourselves to be the WIT-NESS and allowing true, unconditional love, it feels uncomfortable. So, what happens is that we start creating stories again and forming judgments.

Anger is the first line of protection against being hurt or judged. So, we start picking fights or creating chaos, to give reason for the NARRATOR to say, *"I need my armor back. I need the ice layers back. I need to rebuild the callus around my heart. I need to close back up, because it just hurts too much to be the WITNESS."*

That's what's going to happen first for humanity as a whole in this process of choosing to step into the WITNESS. People will get angry and defensive. It will feel easy and convenient to fall back into the familiar reality. But, it's really not. When you're the Tin Man, the Ice Man, or the Callused Scrooge, you're not comfortable. Familiar is not the same as free.

It's hard to be the WITNESS and remain there. The pull of the world is strong, a slippery slope that makes it easy to forget to live in the WITNESS and re-identify with our JUDGE and NARRATOR. But, you can learn how to strengthen the WITNESS in you, so that it doesn't become dormant again.

This is where it's vital to our aliveness to pause, have moments of silence, meditate, pray, and play in joy. These allow space for re-membering and reconnecting with the wholeness of consciousness and the heart space.

It is extremely important that we WITNESS ourselves, that we be WITNESSED by others, and that we connect with a community of people who are remembering how to be in their WITNESS. In this way, we can hold each other strong in love and gentleness, and remind one another when we feel like we're falling apart that we are never really broken. We are only in a phase of letting go of programmed patterns and rebuilding and re-knowing who we are, where we came from, and why we're here.

In my next book, you will learn more about why we came here to be the WITNESS. And, you will learn how to catch yourself when you're forgetting. You will discover how to recognize, actively in the moment, when you are under the overcontrolling influence of the JUDGE and NARRATOR, and reconnect with your WITNESS. Ultimately, you will discover how to embody your WIT-

NESS, through activities and journaling to activate your WITNESS and fulfill your assignment.

You can work with me to understand more about your JUDGE and NARRATOR in a way that enables you to acknowledge them, love them, and co-create with them and the WITNESS.

You came to this life as the WITNESS. Your first assignment is to rediscover how to be that again.

ABOUT THE AUTHOR

Cinthia Veronica Gambino - MSM, SHRM-SCP

Creator of **The ITMYS™ Method**

https://cinthiagambino.com/

Instagram.com/cinthiaveronicamsm
cinthiaveronicamsm@gmail.com

Cinthia Gambino is an immigrant from Mexico and proud of her heritage and culture. She enjoys reading, playing guitar, singing, dancing, cooking and coaching– *not only because it is her passion*– but also because it provides her with the deep fulfillment of being in service to humanity.

Cinthia cherishes deep connections with people who come into her life and loves to see them succeed. Her greatest joy is to help people access the beautiful side of life. She loves connecting with her family, friends, and clients while sharing sacred spaces.

Cinthia currently resides in Philadelphia with her partner Joffre and travels throughout the year to be close to her loved ones whenever she can. Cinthia primarily provides virtual intuitive integration coaching with holistic modalities, through her trademarked Intuitive Leadership Coaching Methodology, **The ITMYS™ Method.** Her services support people in regaining inspiration and re-integration into their lives through the use of new tools.

In addition to being a resource for adults, **The ITMYS™ Method** is also being taught as an adapted curriculum to motivate high school students to achieve their best work, while also creating community in Los Angeles, California.

Cinthia's Full List of Services:

Intuitive Coaching Sessions
1:1 Soul Guidance Sessions
Group Coaching
Integration Coaching for Cacao, Psilocybin, Mescaline and Ayahuasca Ceremonies
The Wish Game Facilitator
Self-Empowerment Events and Retreats
Corporate Culture Trainings
Team Building

Skills and Accolades:

Bilingual (Spanish-English)

Background:

Self Sufficiency Counselor and Goals Trainings Facilitator since 1998
Experienced & Certified HR Professional

Education and Certification:

Hope International University
Bachelor of Science in Human Development with
Emphasis in Counseling
Master of Science in Management
Breakthrough Coaching Certification
Reiki Certification Level 1 and 2
Hypnotherapy Certification
Senior Certified Professional in Human Resources

www.ingramcontent.com/pod-product-compliance
Lightning Source LLC
Chambersburg PA
CBHW020245130626
46549CB00005B/2073